MAYBE MOTHER DID KNOW BEST

THIS IS WHAT WE GOT YOU WITH THE GIFT CERT. JANICE GAVE GREG TO BE USED AT THE NEWS DEPOT. SHE SAID TO ENCLOSE IT WITH HER PICTURES.

DAD
1/17/00

THE 3×4 PICTURES ARE FROM DAVID. THEY ARE GREAT. I'M GOING TO HAVE SOME ENLARGED

MAYBE MOTHER DID KNOW BEST

DID KNOW BEST

Old-Fashioned Parenting the Modern Way

LINDA LEE SMALL

AVON BOOKS NEW YORK

AVON BOOKS, INC.
1350 Avenue of the Americas
New York, New York 10019

Copyright © 1999 by Skylight Press
Interior design by Kellen Peck
Published by arrangement with Skylight Press
ISBN: 0-380-79803-4
www.avonbooks.com

Library of Congress Cataloging in Publication Data:

Small, Linda Lee.
    Maybe mother did know best : old-fashioned parenting the modern
way / Linda Lee Small.
        p.   cm.
    1. Parenting.   2. Parent and child.   3. Child rearing.   4. Child
psychology.   I. Title.
    HQ755.8.S615   1999   99-11098
    649'.1—dc21   CIP

First Avon Books Trade Paperback Printing: April 1999

AVON TRADEMARK REG. U.S. PAT. OFF. AND IN OTHER COUNTRIES, MARCA REGISTRADA, HECHO
EN U.S.A.

Printed in the U.S.A.

OPM   10 9 8 7 6 5 4 3 2 1

This book is dedicated to the memory of my parents, Marcia and Murray Small, who were old-fashioned in the best sense of that word, and for my teenage son, Scott, who continuously forces me to be modern.

✳

Acknowledgments

Special thanks to Meg Schneider and Lynn Sonberg of Skylight Press for their suggestions and guidance; to my agent Agnes Birnbaum of Bleecker Street Associates; and my friend and editor Susan McHenry who always has a sharp blue pencil and an even sharper mind. I am indebted to all the parents and professionals who shared their experiences with me: Julia Ayoub; Maryann Bucknum Brinley; Peter Cohen, Ph.D; Judi Craig, Ph.D; Elizabeth Dince, Ph.D; Antoinette Lynn, Ph.D; Dr. Sanford Mathews; Sal Maugeri; Dennis Meade; Dr. Howard Schlacter; Barbara Sprung; and Kay Willis.

I would particularly like to thank my friend, pediatrician Paula Elbirt, for her wisdom, encouragement, and generosity; and child psychologist Kenneth Condrell who never said no to me—no matter how many times I asked him for his advice.

✳

Contents

ix

✳

Introduction

Not long ago I was at a neighborhood crafts fair. I stopped to say hello to another mother, Jean, whose older son had once been in the same karate class as my son. As Jean and I started to talk, her three-year-old son Josh began to hit her. The more we talked, the more Josh hit. Sheepishly Jean explained, "Oh, he only hits me if I talk to another adult." Hand in hand, Jean and Josh moved on as if the "beating" had never occurred. Another mother who had witnessed the scene came over, and after we agreed (or hoped) we would never indulge such behavior, the same thought occurred to both of us almost simultaneously: Can you imagine Josh getting away with that with OUR parents?

Of course, I couldn't.

Chances are good ole Josh would never have touched his parent in the so-called good old days, and if he had he would have been swiftly dealt with.

Rules, after all, were rules. No matter what. That's what was right about those days. But also wrong.

The Way It Used to Be

We are the children of the generation that lived through World War II and the depression. Our parents were not conflicted about their role as parents. They knew what they had to do. (They certainly would have known what to do with Josh!) Our parents worked hard and, in return, expected a considerable amount of obedience from their children. Their priority was to give us what they decided we needed, not necessarily what we longed for. Our parents paid little attention to the psychological underpinnings of our lives (or theirs for that matter), staying firmly rooted in moral codes, obligations, and practicalities.

Our parents' generation believed children should be seen but not heard. As a result they rarely, if ever, listened to the subtle messages their children sent their way. A child's opinions, feelings, and even fears were often given short shrift, and most situations were drawn in black or white. If you saw a child constantly lollygagging about the house, you assumed he was lazy. (Today we might be more apt to worry that something is upsetting him.) If your child did poorly in school, you jumped to the conclusion that she was irresponsible. (Today you might discover the child has a learning disability.) Troubled kids sent out messages, but they were not accurately received. In general, the psychological life and emotional needs of a child were simply not addressed.

The GOOD, Old Days

On the plus side, old-fashioned parenting meant there was a mother in every house, along with the requisite chicken in every pot, and a car and a bike in almost every garage. You could go down the block, knock on any door, and a mother would appear. Just turn on any '50s sitcom to recall the social landscape.

This was the era when schools were in partnership with parents. Teachers could discipline (and did) as readily as Dad. Every adult was your parent. The extended family included the community and neighbors. As a sixty-year-old recalls of his childhood, "If I was out on the street on a school day, I knew I would be asked repeatedly why I wasn't in school and actually yelled at." And if for some reason your mom wasn't home at 3 P.M., you could knock on almost any door and be invited in for milk and cookies. It indeed "took a village" to raise a child. It's just that then, we took that fact for granted.

The Way It Is, Today

Then the pendulum swung sharply. On the TV screen, Donna Reed and June Cleaver were replaced by the likes of Roseanne or the tart-tongued single mother Grace, Beaver and Wally by bad boys Beavis and Butt-Head. Whereas Beaver worried about a broken bike, today's sitcom kids are just as likely to come from broken homes.

Offscreen, in real living rooms across the country, most parents have been striving to help their children feel respected. Valued. Important. Children, in many ways, are treated as equals.

A well-intentioned approach, but, as we have learned, a misguided one as well.

The not so good, new way

Parents have become much too tentative in the way they wield power over their children. They often confuse the definition of *ally* with that of *friend*. Kids already have the friends they need. Other children.

They do, however, need parents to be on their side. But in a measured way.

Modern parents have been knocking themselves out in an effort to keep their children happy and stress-free. A pediatrician is still reeling over a story she heard in her parents group. It seems that one of the couples was in the process of toilet training their three-year-old. Unfortunately, Seth was routinely having accidents overnight and was waking up wet. They didn't want their son's self-esteem to be damaged, so Dad snuck in when Seth was asleep and put a diaper on him, then Mom snuck in again in the morning and removed the diaper so Seth would be dry. In effect, they didn't want their son, even at this very young age, to experience any failure.

Call the parenting style of the '90s what you will— modern, liberal, progressive, even child-centered. What you can't say is that it has been widely effective.

Time outs are so overused they are losing their bite; parents are confused about how to use them, when to use them, and how long each time out should be. Shielding our children from failure is a bust; it's not only impossible but it's also exhausting and doesn't produce children who succeed. Glorifying our children's every little move has begun to tax, and besides, kids usually can tell when we lavish them with empty and meaningless praise. Talking about "feelings" at every juncture has turned into a dreadful bore for both parent and child. And discussing the motivation for every transgression has become a bar-

ren wasteland of pseudopsychological mumbo jumbo. It
doesn't really matter why the kid stole the cookie. The
point is that he did, and he needs to experience a consequence for his act. Clearly, following the more modern
parenting agenda is not yielding the desired results.

We all want to be enlightened parents, but it's sometimes difficult to see the "enlightenment" at the end of
the dark parenting tunnel. We all want to raise our children the right way, so that they develop a strong moral
sense, solid self-esteem, and dynamic social skills. But
something isn't working. We have not, with all our psychological understanding, saved our children from all
manner of problems. In some cases we are probably caus-
ing them.

The toll of the "new" parenting on parents
It's not good for us, either. Being a parent today is a
stressful and sometimes literally bruising experience. We
are a generation of parents who are worn out from making too many compromises and adjustments: maybe it's
having to create several meals to please several different
palates, or racing to school with left-behind books and
homework. Or maybe it's thinking that all the time we
spend with our children has to be "special."

We know what kind of parenting style we are running
from—parents who didn't spare the rod or worry about
our emotional lives—but we are not quite so sure of what
to put in its place.

We are having tremendous trouble finding the right
balance, and we're beginning to sense the need to borrow
what was effective and combine it with what works now.
We ran from the past, and smacked right into a world of
pop psychology and talk shows with daily pronounce-

ments on the "right" way to raise children. Somewhere we forgot about us, and what we can bring to the table and to our children.

This Is What Works: Old-fashioned Parenting the Modern Way

This book is designed to help parents enjoy parenting again. The advice in this book is based on personal experience, conversations with parents, and interviews with psychologists and pediatricians who explain why these rules *do* work.

Somewhere between the rigid rules of the past and the too lenient ones of the present, we found, just like a modern-day Goldilocks, the ones that are "just right."

We culled through all of the practical wisdom to come up with rules that help parents raise "good" kids—kids with values, character, and solid self-esteem.

We can correct what our parents did wrong (insisting we clean our plates, for example), while acknowledging what they did right (expecting us to take responsibility for our mistakes). There is something to be said for getting back to basics—like putting a value on manners, having regular chores and responsibilities, and respecting adults.

It's time to go back and look at our mothers' basics, even our grandmothers' basics. What's wrong with chicken soup remedies? Scientists have discovered what grandmothers instinctively knew—there really *is* a penicillin-like enzyme in the soup that helps cure the common cold.

This is not to say that there is no longer a place for the more modern insistence on psychological understanding, good communicative conversation, or warm, nonjudgmental love and support. There is no incompatibility between flexible, measured, and empathic parenting and making demands on your child's character.

In fact many of the "just-right" rules in this book are already being practiced; it's just that most parents don't feel confident enough to readily admit it. In a world obsessed with winning and being the best, parents rarely admit to allowing their kids to hand in mediocre work or even letting their kids occasionally feel guilty.

This is a book about sometimes bending rules that are firm, criticizing kids whom you also openly praise, and allowing failures and mistakes while supporting your children's efforts. It's about letting your children taste guilt before the forgiveness, experience the unpredictable as well as the reliable you, and acknowledge sadness believing that happiness is around the bend.

This is a book about embracing the past and the present and settling down into a style that combines the best of both.

In short, this book is about parenting for now. It's a book about acknowledging that, as parents, WE actually might know what's best.

MAYBE MOTHER DID KNOW BEST

✳ **1** ✳

Your Child Does Not Have to Be Numero Uno in Your Life

THE RULE USED TO BE:
Adults always come first.

In the good old days parents always came first. Children often skipped around the edges of their parents' lives and only periodically nudged their way into the forefront. (Think of Nancy and Ronald Reagan, whose children have always appeared to be outsiders.) Typically when Dad arrived home from work, Mom shifted her attention away from the kids to offer the man of the house his ritual slippers, newspaper, and martini. Children knew they were Number Two, so they tried harder *all* the time.

The problem with this model is that it is not good to set up a pattern where children are always either peripheral or an afterthought. This is simply alienating. You want your children to learn that they deserve respect from others, and the first place they can learn that is from their parents.

THE RULE BECAME:
The needs of the child come first.

Parents overreacted to not having enough parental attention paid to them as children. Lately it's as if a large heart is drawn, and parents invite their children permanently in. We are the generation that proudly wears our children on our chests—in a Snugli—and we forget to ever take them off!

Departing from their own parents' often distracted parenting, moms and dads today tell themselves that childhood is so precious that they shouldn't miss one moment of their child's development. So wherever *they* go, their child is sure to follow. These parents constantly tell their child how important she is. But a child who learns to expect the earth to revolve around her is more likely to be a brat.

A prominent Atlanta pediatrician who rarely minces words, Dr. Sanford Matthews, says, "I regularly ask moms, 'Who is more important, you or your child?' and invariably the mom says, 'My child.' " But that's the *wrong* answer. The doctor informs the mother, "The most important person in your life should be *you*. I don't need to talk to you about how to manage your child. He has a genie in a bottle. All he has to do is rub the bottle, and you come out in a big cloud and do whatever he wants." Children may wish for genies, but they need parents.

If you always put your child first, that is what the child comes to expect. One mother explains the downside: "Steven and I were very influenced by a view called 'attachment parenting.' That philosophy emphasizes meeting the needs of the child as much as possible. Beth and I were practically attached at the hip, and I was exclusively devoted to her. But when she was two, I took on a full-time job, and she no longer had me twenty-four hours a day." Mom describes what happened when she went back to teaching elementary school: "Beth regressed in both her speech and toilet training. She had a hard time not being number one in my life all the time."

Parents like Beth's often think that they can't do enough for their children. In other words, they feel that the more they *do* the better parents they are. All that attention on children, however, just creates *more* demanding children.

Little children are by nature self-centered. There is a natural ME, ME, ME stage, genetically engineered by Mother Nature herself. Children think Mommy and Daddy were put on the planet just to meet their demands. But eventually children should come to see that their parents are individuals and also a couple in a marriage. It's the parents' job to help children move the spotlight off of them and to stop promoting the fantasy that parents' sole purpose in life is the fulfillment of their children's needs.

Putting your child first hurts both the child and the marriage. Parents who neglect spending enough time on their marriage find that the fabric of the family frays and can unravel. It's not healthy for your child to be responsible for your joy. Marriages need couple strength. Centered and well-functioning adults need quality time with themselves and other adults.

HERE'S WHAT WORKS:
Your child doesn't always have to be numero uno.

You do not need to be on constant alert, immediately answering every single one of your children's many demands. You must be able to recognize your *own* needs and then be prepared to meet them.

❋ Take time for yourself. You require some time alone. Let your children get used to the idea that Mommy or Daddy, or Mommy *and* Daddy, go to their rooms for privacy. They will learn to tolerate your retreats, and you can gradually increase their duration. If there's a lock on your door, use it, when necessary. Let your kids know that unless it is an emergency, you are not to be disturbed during your own periodic "time outs."

❋ Get support. The honest parent will recognize that no matter how much she loves her children, she can't stand them sometimes and needs to take a break from parenting. Prepare for the time when you will leave your children with others by finding reliable help. Interview sitters, call up their references, and then have the best candidates sit with your children while you are still home. It may take extra time, but it's worth it.

❋ When you do go out without your children, make sure you really leave them behind. A neighbor's daughter just came back from baby-sitting a two-year-old. "You wouldn't believe all the numbers they left me," she says. "The father left me his beeper number, his car phone number, and the number of the restaurant. And they *still* called every fifteen minutes." Don't be like a grown-up ET and continuously phone home. Once you choose a reliable baby-sitter, go out and concentrate on your spouse. This doesn't mean it will be easy the first time you try it; you may even have to peel a little one off your knee in order to exit the front door.

The most important relationship in a family is the one

between mom and dad. Various couples have come up with different strategies to ensure they stay a couple. One mother of four notes: "Hal and I feel that Saturday night should be date night. It is important that we go out together even if our kids have nothing to do. Over the years, we would go out and see that other adults were out with their kids and I'd think, 'Maybe it wouldn't have been such a terrible thing if we took them with us.' But we don't change our policy. Mostly we believe that we come first on Saturday night. We still do."

Whether it's Saturday night or even a family vacation, the fact that parents are a couple can be woven right into your daily lives. Let's say you are doing a fabulous Disney vacation with your kids. Even though it's clearly a family holiday, it doesn't mean that everything should be planned exclusively for the enjoyment of the children. So you might tell the kids in advance, "We are going to do some things just for you kids, like 'Breakfast with Mickey Mouse.' Other times we will eat in grown-up restaurants. We may even get you guys a baby-sitter on Saturday night, so Mom and I can go to Pleasure Island and listen to jazz." This is a way of reminding the kids that even though you are a family, you and your spouse are also adults with adult needs.

It's been said that how the marriage goes, so does the family. Your children need you to have a strong relationship with your mate. Putting yourself first is really doing your children a big favor.

✳ 2 ✳

It's OK for Kids to Be Unhappy

THE RULE USED TO BE:
Being unhappy builds character.

In the old days, kids were simply told how to act. "Don't cry." "Be brave." There was little attention paid to how they were feeling inside. Happiness was not a high-priority goal for anyone in the family.

Consider the running gag in the 1970 movie *Lovers and Other Strangers*. When the actress Diane Keaton, in her debut role, tells her parents she is going to get a divorce, they ask why. She answers, "Because I'm not happy." Her mother turns to her husband and asks, almost incredulously, "Are *you* happy?" When he assures her that NO he isn't, the mother turns again to her daughter and says, "SO why are you divorcing?" All through the movie the long-married spouses assure each other that they are not happy. And they seem to like it that way. They had no expectation of real happiness.

Being unhappy may build character, but it doesn't lead to personal satisfaction. Parents who pay no attention

to their children's unhappiness lose the opportunity to
create a companionable and supportive relationship with
their children. Parents who always let their children bear
the weight of difficult emotions alone risk alienating them.
Children need parents who actively help them find solutions to their unhappiness; otherwise, children won't feel
their parents are ever on their side.

THE RULE BECAME:
My children should always be happy.

Parents tend to respond to their children's every sob as
proof that they are bad parents. Consequently, they do
almost anything to dry their children's tears before they
even appear. Such parents truly fear that even one moment's unhappiness will do significant damage to their
children. This emphasis on putting on a permanently
happy face is in stark contrast to our parents' generation.

Some of this need to keep our children happy comes
from the affluence and indulgence enjoyed by middle-
class American families over the last forty years. We are
a generation proud of our accomplishments. There is a
sense that because we have everything, we should give
everything to our children. But there is a downside to all
this emphasis on being "up." Overindulgence is no certain path to happiness. In the long run, a child who has
become accustomed to having life go his way has no ability to deflect or surmount negative moods and other barri-
ers. As a result, we end up with preschool children whose
days are ruined if they don't get the red crayon when
they want it. Children who have little or no experience
with disappointment or discomfort take it very personally.

Once I watched a mother let her child leave the pediatrician's office and go out into the cold without putting on his overcoat. The boy had just had his finger pricked by the doctor for a routine blood test, and he was resisting getting dressed. Mom was trying to make the child feel better—happier. Because you experienced pain, let's forget about any rules, she was essentially saying. The child should have learned instead, OK, you know what, you got hurt for a few seconds, but it's all over now. Mom is back in control. You may have *felt* like no one was protecting you, but I was. The worst thing you can do is let a child flail about without limits and boundaries. A child needs to learn on a daily basis that life hurts but the parent is there to kiss the boo-boos.

If you wonder how far some parents go to shield their children from any disappointments and hurts, consider the "new" etiquette practiced by some parents at birthday parties. "Gifts don't get opened in front of the kids because when a gift is opened, the kid who gave the gift may want it back!" reports one parent. This mother, who objects to this policy, continues, "I don't understand why we don't just explain to our kids that this is the birthday child's special day and she or he gets to keep the gift. That's the way it is." As a result of this attempt to keep children from getting upset, they never know the true joy of giving.

HERE'S WHAT WORKS:
It's OK for kids to be unhappy.

Children need to experience frustration, disappointments, and unhappiness. You must understand that all children have to learn to hear and deal with "no." The best reason to allow them to be unhappy as children, paradoxically, is that it is the only way they will emerge as happy, fulfilled adults.

If you try to protect a child from every possible problem, you end up with an incompetent child who cannot solve problems or find solutions on his or her own. The same is true if you throw your children to the proverbial lions with no protective gear, always letting a child fend all by herself in times of stress. If you practice either extreme, you end up with the same result: a child without real coping skills.

✳ Let your child experience small doses of frustration. Pediatrician Paula Elbirt, author of *A New Mother's Home Companion*, explains that you need to be guided by your child's developmental stage in helping them cope with frustration in their lives. "Let's start right at the beginning, when you're breast feeding, for example. It is easy to assume that if the child cries she needs to immediately be put on the breast. If the first thing you always do is give them your breast like an extension cord, you are really cheating the child. By not racing to the child, you teach them to tolerate a little bit of frustration. When you come from a distance, you use your voice to say, 'I'm on my way sweetheart. I'm almost here.' You can palpably hear a change in her cry. She knows your voice. When you pick her up and smile at her, she may not even need to be fed." Let's fast forward: By the time your child gets to school there should be regular doses of frustration. This is all preparation for becoming a competent, confident adult. You don't want a child who is defeated by any pressure.

❋ Never feel sorry for your child. Sympathy means suffering along with him—crying with the child, getting into his sadness, being a part of his irrational response to the fact that he has been hurt, pinched, pushed, or deprived. But if he is crying and you are crying with him, nobody gets to the business of integrating that experience and moving on. (If he sobs, hand him a tissue.) It won't permanently hurt his self-esteem if you don't "enter" his feelings. Pediatrician Dr. Sanford Matthews adds, "When your child finds out how sympathetic you are, he is going to take out his violin and make you dance like you have on a pair of magic red shoes. You will never stop dancing until he stops playing, and he's not likely to stop until he's sick and tired of your dancing." This is a hard pattern to break.

❋ Once you acknowledge it's OK for a child not to always be happy, he needs to learn how to BE unhappy. Children often feel out of control when they are distressed, and they need to get used to that feeling. Make it clear early on that just because he is unhappy, he shouldn't try to make everyone else miserable. Say to your child, "I can see you are really unhappy about getting a bad grade on that report, but you are not allowed to yell at me."

Let's say Peter announces that he hates his brother after coming home from a soccer game where he was the goalie but did not manage to block any goals. You can say, "You don't hate your brother, you hate the way the game went." And add, "Remember the legendary Pele had bad days too." You might suggest some activity to Peter to distract him. You are not telling him to cheer up or forget it, just to put it in perspective.

A parent who lives by the principle that all she wants is for her children to be happy will be forever exhausted as she figuratively marches ahead with a broom trying to sweep away all the possible land mines of life. Children need to experience both good *and* bad times.

Parents sometimes think that if they could anticipate every need of their child's and satisfy them before they even had them it would be good for the child. But that's absolutely not true. You want to prepare your children for the reality of living in the world. So they need to know that it may rain on days you were planning a picnic in the park. And your daughter may get a cavity even if she brushes every day. As the kids themselves say: Stuff happens.

✳ **3** ✳

It's OK for Kids to Experience Failure

THE RULE USED TO BE:
Children should do very well in everything they attempt.

Having to excel puts too much pressure on children. No one can do well in everything, so we shouldn't be setting up those kinds of expectations. It's important and humbling for children to know and understand their limitations. If children are expected to do well at everything, they may actually not try to do anything. Growing up just naturally involves frustrations, disappointments, and setbacks. (See previous rule.) Mild suffering *does* in fact help build character.

MORE RECENTLY THE RULE BECAME:
It's bad for my child's self-esteem to experience failure.

This reaction is a corollary to parents' not wanting their child to be unhappy. Parents who feel this way do almost anything to keep their children from experiencing failure.

A doctor relates an experience that pointedly demonstrates how self-protective actions undermine a child's healthy development. The doctor examined a three-and-a-half-year-old who was still in diapers. When asked about the diapers the mom said, "He's not interested in giving them up." Later when the child was out of the room, Mom revealed that her son *had* expressed interest in wearing underwear, but when he wore them, he wet himself almost every time. Mom projected that her son was humiliated by the accidents, so she put him back in diapers as a preventive measure against failure. But what she *really* did was make sure he would not succeed by taking away his incentive to learn to control his bladder. According to the pediatrician, the mother should have been giving her child the message, It's OK that you are wet. Maybe next time, you'll get the hang of this. It will happen one of these times.

Today, many parents try to raise their children in a stress-free environment. When these children do taste their first sip of failure they are often truly devastated.

HERE'S WHAT WORKS:
It's OK for kids to experience failure.

Children really do learn from their mistakes and their failures. Parents can't smooth over *all* the rough edges of life.

But when the bumpy times do occur, we can be there with open arms, kisses, and maybe even Band-Aids. One mother explains, "There's a lot to be said for learning about failure, as a kid, in small measures. The lessons have to be learned at some point in life, and if they are not learned as a kid, they pile up, and you just have to learn them later." It's up to parents to soften the blows without totally eliminating the lessons.

How to Succeed at Failing

❀ Let your children practice failure. Do this by playing card games and board games that rely on luck. They will see in playing War or Trouble that sometimes, no matter what, if you don't get the ace you lose. And then you can let that game go and focus your energies on competing in the next round.

❀ Encourage your child to take risks and try a wide variety of activities. Music, art, sports, theater—different children have different skills. Your child is likely to stumble and fail at some and then find others she is better at. Cara, eleven, did not have much success at sports and was getting quite discouraged at not having an after-school activity she was good at. Invited to a birthday party that featured a magician, Cara was immediately attracted to hocus-pocus. But it still took several how-to books and two weeks at a special magic camp before she developed real sleight of hand. Now she is a budding magician creating her own original card tricks.

❀ Be supportive. Don't lie about your child's skills, but encourage him ("Good try" or "You almost made it") when the going gets rough. Make sure he understands that you are not concerned with how good he is—it's that he tried. "My oldest son insists on playing baseball even though he's not well coordinated," relates a dad. "We know he is often not thrilled with how he plays. Many times he even has disagreements with the coach because he picks someone else to start. But he has learned perseverance. We tell him, 'If you want to play just *do your best.*' " As a wise parent notes, "What's important is that your child puts in real effort and succeeds at improving."

❋ Redefine *failure*. If you personally define winning as giving it your best shot even if you miss the target, then your kids are more likely to hang in and try. "My son John is not good at basketball, but he loves it," explains one father. "There's no way he's going to make the team at school. But every year I encourage him to try out because he wants to. We both know full well he will probably not make the team." In this house John's efforts are *never* described as *failing*: "He hasn't succeeded at making the team just yet."

❋ Respond in a positive way to a child who fails but tried. If you show disappointment or disapproval, your child will likely feel defeated. So your daughter doesn't make the debating team; or your son struck out every time he was up at bat; and your other daughter got an F on her science test. What's important is to find out what your child can do to improve. (So maybe your daughter needs to come up with a different after-school activity to replace the debating team; your son needs to practice more with his older sister, the batting champ; and your other daughter needs to sign up for

science tutoring.) You don't want failure to be imbued
with severe consequences. If a child is really fearful of
failing, he may just give up.

✳ Be a good role model. "Let your kids know that you
sometimes fail," says one mother, who gives as an example, "I took a series of tennis lessons and I just
didn't have good hand/eye coordination. I let the kids
know I just 'tanked' as a tennis player. I didn't want
them to think I wasn't playing because I didn't like the
game. It's important for them to know I tried it and I
was really lousy." And she adds: "On the other hand,
my family knows I'm a great Scrabble player. I beat
them all the time."

Kids who can gracefully fail, win by developing courage. Parents should see courage as the ability to hang in
there when the going gets tough. We want our children to
know they can't get a gold, or even silver, medal in every
activity they try. Sometimes coming in *last* can even be
classified as a triumph, and not a failure, if you overcame
adversity just to get out of the starting block.

❈ 4 ❈

Children Don't Need a Gold Medal for Everything They Do

THE RULE USED TO BE:
It is not necessary to praise children at all.

Our parents often didn't take the time to stop and praise their children, sometimes for fear it would give the child a swelled head. And when they did praise it was only to recognize major accomplishments. ("It's nice that you won first prize at the science fair.") Children who never received gold stars for any reason rarely felt appreciated or special. This generation of parents rarely caught their kids being good and focused instead on correcting them when they were bad. By not recognizing the value of praise as a motivator they lost many opportunities to reinforce good behavior.

THE RULE BECAME:
Praise children for every little thing they do to boost their self-esteem.

It's OK for our kids to feel special, but it's not necessary to go overboard praising everything they do or say. One of the problems with today's child-centered parenting is that parents think they can simply *give* children self-esteem by always praising and saying nice things to them.

A popular bumper sticker asks, "Have you praised your child today?" One dad observes, "I'm tempted to shout back at the sticker, 'No, not if he doesn't deserve it.' "

A teacher warns against a current trend: "I've seen kids come back from kindergarten wearing signs that read, 'I'm the best. I'm wonderful.' The problem is that the child hasn't done anything really special all day."

Most experts criticize the common practice today of giving awards, medals, citations, and the like to anyone who simply shows up for any competition. Children who know they did nothing to earn it realize how little such an award means; other children begin to expect to get prizes for everything. The truth is that excessive praise produces the opposite of what is desired: children with low self-esteem.

HERE'S WHAT WORKS:
Children don't need a gold medal for everything they do.

What you want is a child who appreciates himself and doesn't need someone else to tell him he is good and terrific. A child will develop this solid sense of himself if he hears *accurate* praise from other people and then internalizes it.

The truth is that self-esteem has to be "earned" through acquiring skills that represent some achievement—learning how to tie shoes, for example, or reading a longer book.

Praiseworthy Actions

✳ What children need is acknowledgment that makes them feel loved and valued. ("You are a really neat kid. I love having you ride with me to the store because you are good company.")

✳ Recognition from others for a job truly well done builds self-esteem. Praise should be accurate, specific, and sincere. When you praise a child for cleaning up her room properly, or for how nicely she combed her hair when she usually doesn't comb it at all, there was something she did to earn your praise.

✳ Don't give marshmallow praise that has no substance. "You are the best," for example, is not effective praise. Your child is smart enough to know she is not really the most beautiful or the most terrific kid in the world. If you say, "You are so wonderful," your child should respond, "Tell me five ways in which I am so wonderful." Be prepared to answer that follow-up question or don't make the empty comment.

❋ 5 ❋

Kids Don't Need to Express an Opinion on Everything

THE RULE USED TO BE:
Kids should be seen but not heard.

With the phrase "You should be seen but not heard," parents often devalued and dismissed children's opinions and feelings. Kids felt as if they didn't count at all.

When parents didn't include children in any decision making, children kept their thoughts to themselves and rarely had meaningful conversations with adults. A psychologist now in his sixties recalls of his own childhood, "When I was about ten, I once told a friend of the family that sometimes I felt sad and would go to the park. The friend reacted by laughing out loud and saying, 'Kids don't have any reason to be sad.'" As the psychologist says today of that adult's reaction, "He thought it was funny to think that kids could have real feelings. But they do."

THE RULE BECAME:
Kids should be seen AND heard.

So-called progressive parents welcome children into every conversation and treat their child's every utterance like pearls of wisdom. As a result, it's not uncommon to meet children who think it's OK to speak their minds whenever they feel like it, no matter what. Parents go to such lengths to make sure children express themselves that they actually allow them to be rude and intrusive. We now have little kids saying, "I don't have to listen to you" or "You can't make me" or even "Shut up." Children easily go from thinking everything they say is important to thinking what YOU say isn't.

Our children should not be encouraged to think that just because we ask their opinions at home, this will happen in the "real" world. More often than not, they will be in for a rude awakening. A psychologist shares this story: At home, Susan, 16, was always invited to join every conversation and participate in all decisions that affected her life. At school, Susan was punished for turning in a textbook late. The principal announced: "All students with late books get lunch detention today." Susan's book was just half a day late and other students had books out for as long as three weeks. An A student, Susan was humiliated to be given lunch detention and declared, "That's just for losers." She tried to negotiate a different punishment. When the principal refused, Susan simply dug in and said, "That punishment is just not right for me." She wound up getting a stiffer punishment for her troubles.

A currently popular but misguided notion is: It will damage my child's self-esteem if she doesn't participate in the decisions that affect her. As a result the child gets to give her opinion. All the time! The consequences can run from the ridiculous to the disastrous. One parent sits down with his son at the end of every school year at a private school and inquires, "Which teacher do you think you would like?" This puts the child on the same level as the parent. He is being misled to think he is an equal to the adult in his life.

HERE'S WHAT WORKS:
Kids don't need to express an opinion on everything.

It's not necessary to always ask for our children's opinions or to inquire, "Well, how do *you* feel about that?" Nor should you allow your children to express themselves in every situation. When one mother finally grew frustrated at her ten-year-old daughter's constant need to discuss parental decisions, she said, "Honey, please stop talking." "Honey" then responded with a discourse on her "first amendment right to free speech." This mother wished she had long ago learned to use the phrase she had deliberately banned from her parental repertoire: "Because I said so!"

❊ Let kids know there will be a time and a place for them to express themselves. Children can be vibrant and full of ideas and thoughts. It makes them proud when you ask, "What do you think about this?" But they need to be considerate of other people's feelings. If the child is at the table and excitedly interrupts an adult because she has something to say, *you* interrupt: "Excuse me, but I don't believe your aunt has finished what she was saying. But we would like to hear what you have to say when she finishes."

✳ You have to balance the child's need to know against the parents need to simply get things done. A single mother of three admits: "I have had to work this out over time. Now I say, 'I'd like to know what you think about this.' I let them know I may not do what they say, but I am curious about their opinion." This mom once made the difficult decision, shortly after her divorce, to give away the family dog "Fluffy" without telling the kids; they were devastated and angry at her. Three years later, she handled a similar situation more effectively. Since they were about to move to an apartment that didn't accept dogs, she told them in advance at a family meeting that "Fluffy II" had to go. "I explained that Fluffy was going to the country and she was going to live with Grandma in the woods. I asked if there were any questions. My youngest paused and then said seriously, 'Mom, is Grandma a dog or a real grandma?' " Once I assured my son that Fluffy was going to live with my mother, he was just fine with the news. This time the kids could handle it."

Parents have made it seem that *all* time is family time, and therefore children feel they have permission to intrude with their opinions. Help children define what *is* family time and when it is appropriate for them to express themselves. Set aside time for listening to your children and routinely updating your family. This gives you the opportunity to give them information they need ("We are going to the zoo today, and we will eat before we go"), as well as a chance to hear what is on their minds ("If we are going to the zoo, can I take pictures with my new camera?"). If there are regular "family news updates," your children are less likely to feel alienated or left out.

✳ **6** ✳

It's Not Necessary to Give Child Options Every Single Time

THE RULE USED TO BE:
Parents always set the agenda.

Since the child's opinion wasn't valued, parents made all the choices about what the child would wear, eat, and do. But all children need some measure of independence and control over their lives. Kids who are never given any options feel powerless. And contrary to the popular saying that power corrupts, some experts believe that powerlessness is what truly corrupts and makes people feel lousy about themselves.

THE RULE BECAME:
Parents present their children with options and choices.

There is an epidemic of parents giving their children endless choices when it is not appropriate. There are situations when the parent should be in charge. A pediatrician recalls the time she walked into the examining room to hear a mom asking her young son if it was OK if the doctor gave him a shot. The doctor recalls, "I said, 'I'm not giving him that option. If YOU are let me know because then I'll come back when you decide.' " In another similar situation, the doctor impatiently asked the parent, "Aren't you going to let me give this child a shot because it's a life-saving vaccine?" Her response: "Well yes. But I want to give him the feeling he has a choice." But this is a deception. (In this case, the child should have no choice, and he needs to know that, just as he needs to learn that there will be many situations in life where even an adult has no choice.) The child doesn't need to give his permission. What he does need is for his parent to say, "You need a shot today to keep you strong and healthy. It will be over quickly."

Often the scenario continues with the parent now asking the child WHERE he wants the shot: "Do you want to be on the table, or in my arms, or in the doctor's arms?" As the frustrated doctor says, "The child is better off in his parent's lap unless you want the shot to end up in his earlobe." What all these questions accomplish is "an amazing prolonging of pain."

A psychologist notes that when children come into her office with significant problems, the parent often thinks its OK if the kid doesn't want to come back. As the doctor says, "Would you give your child the option to come back to a dentist if he had cavities? The work isn't done, but parents have accepted the premise that the child has the same right to make decisions as I do."

Parents today often use options as a substitute for setting limits, but kids really do need rules and structure. "The thing that makes me the most crazy in my office is when I listen to parents negotiate with their children and get outmaneuvered," observes a pediatrician, who relates the following scenario:

"We have to go now, Billy. You have to let other kids play with toys. Put on your red coat."

"I want to play with toys."

"If we play with toys for just a few minutes, then you'll put on your red coat and we can go."

"I'm not wearing my red coat. I don't like it. We're going to stay and play with toys."

The doctor sums it up: "The really sad part is that the parent agrees and winds up staying in the office with Billy."

HERE'S WHAT WORKS:
It's not necessary to give children options in every single situation.

It's not an insult to the child's integrity for you to be in charge. Many parents seem to think that nothing short of full disclosure about what will happen next is deceptive. Billy's pediatrician has even heard parents *begging* their children to forgive them because they didn't warn them in advance that they might get a shot. ("Please, honey, I didn't know. Should we come back another day?") Life is full of surprises—not all of them good (remember chapters 2 and 3). Teach your child to roll with the punches and, yes, the pinches too, and get on with it.

✳ It's OK to offer children limited options about certain things. For example, your seven-year-old son is about to race out the door to school dressed in torn jeans and a T-shirt. Today is also picture day at school. You don't get into a long discussion of how he is dressed. You just bring out two shirts and say, "Which would you like to wear today?" Period. (But don't try this with a teen!)

✳ Make sure *you* are in the decision-making seat. A parent who gives her child reasonable options, but remains in control, shares her techniques: "We use options as a technique since she hit the terrible twos, when it was so difficult to get her to do anything. We lead her through a progression that gets her ready for preschool. Maybe she doesn't want to go to preschool. We won't wangle over that. *She has to go.* We do ask her, 'Do you want to put on your sneakers or your sandals?' We never give her more than two choices to get her to go along with the program. She's in control of some issues like whether she wants peanut butter or tuna in her lunch box. Sometimes she says, 'I want Fruit Loops.' And we just say, 'No.' I may say, 'I wish I could let you eat that all the time. I wish I could eat Fruit Loops all the time, but we can't. That's only for a treat.' Usually, 'I wish I could do that too' appeases her because it helps her know that I empathize."

✳ Understand that having too many options often con-
fuses children. A child may even make a choice without
consciously considering the pros and cons of the alternative if he has not yet learned this skill. A young child
is not developmentally ready to learn to make distinc-
tions. For example, it's been noted that small children
often choose by numerical order. A preschool teacher
explains, "I always tell parents if you want your child
to choose a particular item, just mention it last. If you
say, 'Do you want to wear the blue or the red shirt?'
nine times out of ten, he will chose the red shirt. It has
to do with memory." So a young child making real
choices is really just an illusion.

Children learn to make good judgment calls based on
real life experiences and a sense of fairness, constancy,
and commitment. It's not necessary to have a Socratic dialogue over every detail of your child's life.

✳ **7** ✳

Forget It, You Can't Always Be Fair

THE RULE USED TO BE:
I give my child what I think he needs.
(Or, What's fairness got to do with it?)

In the past, busy parents were mostly concerned that their children got what they needed (food, shelter, clothing), not necessarily what they wanted. ("Mom, I would love that brown sweater with the leather trim.") Parents made unilateral decisions about what each child was to get, and often the oldest was bestowed the biggest share and the best of everything. Older brothers, in particular, always seemed to be showered with attention and material things, while the younger one was often left with feelings of envy and a real blow to his self-esteem ("I must be worth less than my brother because I always get less"). The concept of fairness was rarely addressed: It just wasn't a priority because parents rarely considered the impact that "unfairness" would have on their children.

THE RULE BECAME:
I go out of my way to treat my children exactly the same at all times.

Parents seem almost obsessed with making sure each child receives equal amounts of love, energy, and "goodies."

This parenting style is based on the widely held misconception that good parents are always fair. Parents incorrectly assume that by being fair they will be satisfying their children, but tit-for-tat parenting just oversensitizes children to the issue of inequality. The result is that children end up torturing and hounding parents with their scorekeeping. While some children feel aggrieved, others may develop a false sense of position and importance. ("I must really be special. I'm much younger, but I get *just* what my older brother gets.")

There are too many kids walking around today with calculators in their brains keeping track of who got what. They develop the appalling habit of hassling over every crayon, or cookie, or whatever they feel should be coming to them. And they feel victimized whenever things don't go their way. Kids can get very petty: On a long car trip one little girl complained bitterly that her brother was looking out of "her" window.

HERE'S WHAT WORKS:
Forget it. You can't always be fair.

Sooner or later your child will say, "You're not fair. You're never fair. He always gets to do what he wants and I don't." It's the rare parent who has not heard this accusation. Understand this: The issue of fairness is really a screen for sibling rivalry. The child is usually asking for more love and attention.

When a child says "You're not fair," it puts parents on the defensive. But as we've seen, the parent who tries to deal with "just desserts" too literally only creates a more demanding youngster. ("He sat next to you three times yesterday, and I only sat next to you twice. So it's my turn now.") Parents are often confused about handling complaints like this because of the unwarranted fear that their child may grow up feeling rejected or unloved.

The next time your child charges you with the crime of unfairness sit him down and say, "Understand that life is not always fair, but let me explain how *I* am fair." Answer with plain facts. You could say, "You are five. You have an earlier bedtime than your nine-year-old brother, you have a smaller allowance, and you aren't yet allowed to go around the block on your bike or stay over at a friend's house like he can. Your brother definitely has more privileges because he is older, but he also has more responsibilities. I expect him to do an hour of homework each night with very little help from me. He also has more chores. You don't have to do those extra things because you are younger. And I give you more help with whatever you do. I help you clean your room, and I help you with your reading. So I'm fair."

Here you are painting a clear picture for your children that older means more privileges, but also more work and less help. Younger equals fewer privileges but less work and more help from Mom and Dad. This explanation makes sense.

Parents will have to devise their own scales to work

out the balance between siblings. Sometimes it's just easier to start out treating kids the same. As one father explains, "Both Allan, twelve, and Zeke, nine, get the same allowance of $5.50. I didn't agonize over that too much. I suppose one could argue that Allan should get extra." On paper it looks equal, but in reality this dad makes sure that Allan, who has more needs, ultimately gains access to sufficient resources: "We have this earning and matching-funds-system where we figure out how to meet his needs." Currently Allan wants a drum set, so he and the family are coming up with ways for him to earn the money for the drums and for his lessons. This dad sums it up: "I've taught my sons to focus on working toward what they want, and not to be concerned with what the other brother has."

❋ Resist the temptation to always even the score between your children. Don't buy into your child's vision of fairness; you can always point out that there are times when one has a privilege the other doesn't and vice versa. One father says, "I tell my children, 'Everyone gets different things at different times, so stop complaining.' "

❋ Try to set up equitable rules, but understand that *whatever* you do children will still find a way to criticize. One mother of eight explains, "We had three bedrooms that had to be shared by two or three kids and one small bedroom that only one child could sleep in. The single bedroom became the room of the child in the house who was sixteen." There were still complaints: "It's not fair. I had the use of the room one month less than my sisters."

⁕ Obviously you need to maintain sensitivity to the ebb and flow of real life. When emergencies and exceptions crop up, all bets are off. A mother explains, "Out of necessity my children learned that if one child was sick, that's who got ninety percent of my attention." If one child is having a particularly hard time because her friend just moved away, she knows she can count on getting extra hugs and more attention at home. In general, kids should feel that they get what they need.

So the next time your daughter comes home with a big goody-bag from a birthday party, and her younger sister complains, agree, "You're right, life is not fair." This should become your mantra: The world doesn't turn on the rules of fairness. You can say, "In this family, we will *try* to be fair." But point out that it is not possible to be fair on a short-term, moment-to-moment basis; it should all balance out over the long haul in a cooperative family atmosphere.

✳ **8** ✳

You Can't Mandate Sleep

THE RULE USED TO BE:
It's 7:30. Lights out. Goodnight.

Our parents simply kissed us, tucked us in, and turned out the lights. If you were afraid of the dark, there were no Disney character-shaped night-lights. There were no night-lights at all. If you were afraid of monsters under the bed, you had to pray they *stayed* under the bed, since it was the rare parent who would take the time to show you that the monster-hiding places were empty. If you had nightmares, they were yours to deal with. You knew you were expected to stay in bed. Parents often wanted kids in bed early so that they could get on with their lives.

A big problem with this routine was that children were supposed to just turn off like the light! But this belief failed to recognize the fact that kids don't just automatically wind down.

THE RULE BECAME:
Bedtime is a very complicated ritual with parents constantly begging and cajoling children to get to sleep.

Here are some common mistakes today's overly anxious parents make:

* ❋ They get into the habit of lying down with their youngster each evening to help him fall asleep.

* ❋ They let their child fall asleep in their bed and then carry him into his own bed. (If he does wake up, he finds himself in a "strange" place.)

* ❋ They rush into the child's room if he wakes during the night and then play with him.

* ❋ They don't set up a pleasurable bedtime ritual.

Understand there is a strong connection between overindulging a child and encouraging sleep problems.

HERE'S WHAT WORKS:
You can't mandate sleep.

You simply can't will a kid to go to sleep. Children go to sleep when they are tired, not necessarily when *you* are tired. So going to bed can easily turn into a power struggle.

Parents often feel so guilty if a child cries for any reason that they have trouble getting and keeping a child in bed. Kids today are rewarded for not going to sleep by getting to spend time with their parents. They think,

"If I'm good at this, I can keep Mommy or Daddy in my room forever, and that way I get to stay up." Instead of winding down, we are winding up our children and actually inspiring them to stay up.

Let your children know what time they are expected to be in bed. Go through any bedtime routines you have, and then shut the door. (Leave a night-light on, if necessary.)

You can't command sleep, but you do have a right to set behavioral limits. For instance, you can say, "No, you can't come out of your room. I want you to stay in bed until morning. Play with some toys or read with a light on, but the rest of the house is off limits." You can get a wandering child to wander back to his bedroom by making sure that being out of his room isn't pleasurable. When he comes out of his room, don't offer any extras to coax him back in—no juice, kisses, bedtime stories, or conversation. Just repeat "It's time for bed, now."

You can also teach a very early riser to look at a clock and see, for example, that when the number is 7 it means it's OK to get Mommy or Daddy. Some parents have learned the hard way to put an index card over the last numbers of a digital clock—otherwise the child may come out when it's 5:27.

※ Help your child become accustomed to noise by allowing normal household sounds during naptime or bedtime.

※ Make sure you leave your child before he has fallen asleep.

※ Don't use your own bed as a pacifier and then carry a sleeping child back to his room.

❋ If your child cries at night, look in on him, but make it a matter-of-fact visit.

❋ Don't bring your child into your bed unless he is really sick.

❋ Do not use your child's bed as a place to put him for punishment.

❋ Encourage his attachment to a "blanky" or stuffed animal.

❋ Enjoy your child during the day so that you don't feel you "owe" him time when he cries at night.

Some lucky parents get away with "Lights out, goodnight, don't let the bedbugs bite." Others have to devise more complicated bedtime routines. The bottom line is that parents shouldn't be sleep deprived. Establish rules and stick with them, so that your child will eventually learn how to get the Sandman to visit him nightly.

✳ **9** ✳

If Your Child Doesn't Like the Menu, She Doesn't Have to Eat

THE RULE USED TO BE:
Clean your plate.

It was once common for mothers, who were usually in exclusive charge of the kitchen, to urge children to finish each and every morsel on their plate. If the child didn't eat, the mother had somehow failed.

Guilt played a heavy role at dinnertime. Reminding their offspring about starving children on the other side of the world, mothers frequently threatened to ship uneaten food to India or China. (A friend of mine wanted to know when her mom would have the time to pack it up, while an even more skeptical diner demanded, "Name two people you sent it to.") The prevailing wisdom (which never really made sense) was that as long as *any* child, anywhere in the world, could be going without food, we had an obligation to eat everything that was put in front of us.

As a result, dinnertime was often drawn out, and the act of dining was downright unappetizing as children were made to eat simply to obey their parents. Typically a child was not allowed to leave the table until she cleared her plate. A child could end up sitting at the table staring at cold oatmeal while the rest of the family were sitting down to a hot lunch. This clean-plate policy also led to a generation of overfed children who habitually ate long after their stomachs were full.

THE RULE BECAME:
What would you like on your plate?

This solicitous generation of parents is overly focused on children enjoying their food, but they are still committed to clean plates at the end of the meal. In a world full of choices, mothers are like personal chefs customizing meals for different picky eaters. ("I created this chicken with peanut dish for Lizzie, who is on a high-protein diet, and this pasta dish is for your brother, who is currently carbo-loading.")

Guilty parents who are not home as much as they would like worry that their children are undernourished psychologically, and transfer their anxieties to a focus on food. Children receive a lot of attention for not eating or being picky. Talk about so-called power breakfasts: There are kids who are regularly offered six different cereals, or asked "Would you like granola, with a cornucopia of fresh seasonal fruit?"

HERE'S WHAT WORKS:
If your child doesn't like the menu, she doesn't have to eat.

Make sure that the dining room table doesn't turn into a battleground. You don't want to be constantly begging, "Please, honey, just take one more bite." Nor should you be threatening, "You can't leave the table until you have eaten everything on your plate."

The mother of Janet, a picky eater, describes what dinnertime is like at her house: "The other kids have left the dinner table, but Janet is still playing with her food. I can feel myself getting really angry as I sit begging her to eat just a little more. But I don't want to turn into my mother and make her finish everything on her plate." It's time for Janet's mom to adjust her attitude to develop strategies that work. Otherwise, Janet will continue to hold her mother hostage to the dining room table.

Let your kids know that dinnertime will *always* be over after a certain amount of time, and once the dishes are cleared away, the kitchen will be officially closed. Janet should know that even if she has eaten only one forkful of her mashed potatoes, her plate will be removed promptly when the dinner hour is over. Make it clear to all picky eaters that there will be no more food until the next meal. You must be consistent. If you give in and offer more food, make sure it is not particularly appealing—maybe just a slice of bread or cereal. Don't be surprised if your child announces she is starving and launches into an Academy Award–worthy performance complete with tears. If she does, just hand her an apple and a tissue.

The point is that kids can't always eat what they want,

when they want it. Respond to special requests with "I am not a short-order cook." (Borrow from the model of large families. As one woman who grew up with six brothers says wryly, "In my house it was survival of the fastest. No one much cared if you liked what was served.")

There are many creative and practical solutions for the so-called picky eater. Let's say this month your son has announced he will only eat "white food": stock up on white bread, white cheese, potatoes, and let it be; if your daughter refuses to eat the hamburger because it has a "crack," then fix it by covering the crack with ketchup; if your kid routinely screams if the vegetables "bump" into the potatoes on his plate, just buy him a plate with compartments. Some kids just naturally have specific food preferences, and others are not very exploratory about food.

❋ *Don't* get into the habit of praising them ("Oh it's so terrific that you cleaned your entire plate") or they will eat even when they are not hungry.

❋ *Don't* overwhelm them with choices.

❋ *Don't* get into the pattern of cooking separate meals for different members of the family.

❋ *Do* create weekly menus (with your children's input) and stick to them.

❋ *Do* make sure that mealtime is for meals—no watching TV, no reading at the table. And mealtime should not be the platform for airing squabbles.

You want your children to understand that *they* are responsible for whether they eat. That's why it's even OK for kids to go to bed without dinner now and then. (This is not a throwback to the days when kids were sent to bed hungry as a punishment.) If you serve your child dinner but *she* chooses not to eat, you can say, "I'll try to prepare some of your favorite meals every week, but otherwise you can pick and choose from what is on the table."

※ **10** ※

Make Sure Your Child Has Responsibilities and Chores

THE RULE USED TO BE:
These are your chores and you do them. Period.

Chores were often rigidly doled out with little give or take. We inherited our work ethic from the days when many Americans lived on a family farm, where it was essential to get up early and tend to the land. There was also a legacy from the harsh urban realities of life many years ago, when little kids labored in sweatshops as part of a low-wage workforce. Yesterday's rigid parceling out of chores trained children for adult work responsibilities but gave short shrift to their other developmental needs.

Many of us vividly recall just what it was like carrying out our childhood chores, and we regularly regale our children with war stories. "Boy, are my kids tired of hearing what I had to do," admits one dad. "I was responsible for keeping the basement and the garage clean, mowing the lawn, and doing my share of the dishes. And I walked a mile to school carrying my tenor saxophone. Kids don't even walk to school anymore. I had to do a lot."

THE RULE BECAME:
My child is so busy. It's OK if he doesn't (always) do his chores.

The view that children were just short adult workers in training was replaced with the view that the preserve of childhood should be a magic kingdom. The generally accepted notion that everyone in the household had to work gradually shifted to the sense that kids were, after all, just kids and should be allowed to play.

The same parent who recounts the long list of chores he took on in his youth complains about the struggle he has with his own children over household tasks: "We're not as successful with delegating responsibilities around the house as with some other stuff. Each kid has basic chores. They aren't a lot compared to what I did, but we are always nagging them to get them done."

Parents today who understand the value of chores still often conspire with their kids to find escape hatches. They easily excuse their children: "Part of the problem is that I have a housekeeper who is there to pick up, so my kids leave stuff around the house. I don't make them make their beds, because their beds are really hard to make. They have a bunk with a trundle bed, a middle bed, and a top bed. It's hard to tuck in the sheets and covers." Many parents today believe that a child should have only one job—school. Naturally this opens the door for kids to regularly evade their chores by claiming they have homework.

If there are no consequences for sloughing off chores, children will regularly squirm their way out of doing them. ("I have band practice." "I'm tired." "I did that yesterday.")

HERE'S WHAT WORKS:
Make sure your child has responsibilities and chores.

It's time to go back to assigning chores to children and insisting they carry out their responsibilities. From the time a child is little she should know she is part of a family and that families pitch in to work together. Assigned chores should, of course, be age appropriate: Little children can take care of little tasks like picking up their toys, and bigger kids can obviously accomplish more.

Frank, the father of three girls ages 3 through 9, explains that all of his daughters have work assignments. He feels strongly that doing their chores makes the kids feel good about themselves: "In this house, we have chores big time. Kay, who is nine, has the longest list: clean room, keep desk clean, keep closet neat, make bed, brush teeth, brush hair, take bath. Put things away. Get homework checked. Put clothes away in closet. Alice, age six, has a shorter list, and the youngest, Cassy three, has an even shorter list, but she has one too." In this house they get bonus points as they complete their chores. Eventually they get money for their points, and they each put it in their own ginger ale bottle.

❋ Give children some options about which jobs they do, but the basic philosophy should be, If you live here, you help in this house. Therefore, children should never routinely get away with not doing their chores— even if they *do* have a big vocabulary test tomorrow.

※ Establish routines, but allow some flexibility about when chores are done. There are chores that can wait, and then there are those that can't. One mom is clear about the difference and where she is willing to bend. "My son has to feed the cats before he goes to school. I don't want to hear why he can't. The cat will be hungry. But on Wednesdays, my other son has to go around the house and put all the trash from the wastepaper baskets into one big garbage bag. I prefer he does it early, but if he wants to do it later I can live with that. The garbage can wait, but the cats can't."

※ If your child balks at performing household duties, you might draw up a clear contract with him about exactly WHAT is to be done, and WHEN it is to be done.

※ Some parents reward compliance with privileges. You might enlist your child's help on what it would take to get him to comply. Make sure it is realistic. (If a teen promises to clean his room if you get him his own phone, forget it. It is more reasonable to negotiate to increase the amount of time he can spend on the phone.)

※ Parents could also reward noncompliance with specific consequences. A parent who has been there explains how it works: "Sometimes my daughter would get really busy and her chores wouldn't get done. We'd finally say, 'Look, if you want to go out Saturday night, you have to finish this stuff by Saturday night.' That always worked."

✳ *Warning*: Moms have a tendency to be critical of the way household chores are done. Many children quickly learn that if they do a lousy job they get rewarded by not having to do it at all, so mothers need to set less exacting standards.

All play and no work doesn't help children develop a sense of responsibility. Chores shouldn't be viewed as punishment but rather as the job you do for your family. Make sure your children feel that they are appreciated for what they contribute, and teach them to take pride in being part of the team.

11

Manners Are Important Because through Them We Express Our Respect for, and Sensitivity to, Others

THE RULE USED TO BE:
Manners need to be impeccable.

Too many rules about proper behavior made children feel like puppets being pulled by parental strings. Our parents may have put too much emphasis on appearances, but their monitoring children's behavior was not entirely all a bad thing. Children understood they were expected to be polite to adults ("Yes, ma'am," "No, sir"). Often our attention was focused on what appeared to be superficial details like which fork to use at a formal dinner, but it is important to master some skills, like looking adults in the eye and shaking hands when you are introduced to people.

THE RULE BECAME:
Manners are old-fashioned, unimportant.

Manners have been so devalued and underappreciated
that people are actually surprised when others are polite
and courteous. We may not like our children's manners,
but we aren't effective in teaching them. Parents who have
little time with their children to begin with and don't
want to be negative often back off and give kids watered-
down responses to poor manners. ("Please don't talk with
your mouth full" is followed by the child still being asked
a question.) Parents who don't make manners a priority
rarely teach children even basics like good table manners.

Today's parents are often the role models their ill-
mannered children follow. They frequently display a lack
of respect for people and property (just think of all the
adults who yell and give the finger to drivers), as if they
are saying it's OK to be rude. As one principal notes,
"When I interview teachers on their views on today's children and manners, I get the response 'It's non-existent.'
And their parents aren't much better."

HERE'S WHAT WORKS:
Manners are important because
through them we express our respect for,
and sensitivity to, others.

A practical emphasis on good manners teaches children
to be thoughtful and considerate of others. Everyone likes
to be treated with respect. No one wants to step on a
discarded wad of old chewing gum, or be screamed at in

traffic. When you are entering a building loaded down with packages, it's a relief to have someone offer to open the door.

People are attracted to other people with good manners, so children should be taught that how they act affects their friendships. "Over the years I have seen many children who were unhappy because they had a difficult time making and keeping friends," notes a child psychologist. "The one thing all these friendless children had in common was a total lack of manners. I start by teaching them how to say 'please' and 'thank you' and how not to grab the crayons and not to burp. This is how I help children who are loners become popular."

✳ Explain to your child why manners are important. We may have backed off from formal ritual behavior, but courtesy and consideration are attractive in other people. No one wants to be around someone who grabs the cookies off the plate before anyone else can reach for one, or who blows his nose into his sleeve.

✳ Understand that teaching manners takes time, attention, and patience, particularly if you are correcting children with poor manners.

Note the following real conversation between a six-year-old and her aunt:

Jenny: I want to see that photo now.

Tess: Excuse me. I'm looking at it. When I'm done I will give it to you.

Jenny: I said, I want it now.

Tess: Jenny, that's rude. I don't like that one bit.

Jenny: Can I please see it when you're done?

Tess: Absolutely. You know why? Because you said "please" and you were considerate of my feelings.

※ Reinforce good manners by being a good role model. "I hope I show my kids through my own behavior how to be respectful towards other people," says one father. "For example, when our carpool buddy is here in the morning I remind them, 'Let's be respectful of John, who has to get to work, and be ready to go.' "

※ Give your child both positive and negative feedback about her manners. "My son grew up in a home where it was important to be polite and respectful. When he wasn't polite, I corrected him, and he knew I was displeased," explains a mother. "If he saw a neighbor with a bundle, he knew that I expected him to offer to help. He also knew I expected good manners from his friends. I didn't like it if friends walked in and just opened up the refrigerator. If a boy came over for dinner and then got up afterwards like a prince, I would say in a casual way, 'Go on back to the table and get your plate,' and I would never have to correct that kid again. He would know in my house these were the rules."

※ It's never too late. A stepmother, Liz, explains how she brought rude behavior to the attention of her step-grandchildren: "When we would visit, the first thing they would say is, 'Did you bring a present? What did you bring us?' " The first time Liz had them alone, she took them out for a Happy Meal and explained, "When grandpa and I come it's not good manners to ask for a gift. If we choose to bring a gift, we may. But you shouldn't ask for it." Liz recalls that the children were thoughtful while they digested their Big Macs and her criticism. The five-year-old looked up and asked very seriously, "What if I forget?" The seven-year-old said to him, "Don't worry, *I'll* remind you." It worked. These basically nice kids just needed to hear what good manners were all about.

Everyone judges an individual by her behavior. If you have poor manners it will be counted against you. It's just more pleasant to be around people who are considerate. As one dad sums it up: "I think manners help our chaotic life be more in balance."

12

Let Your Children Do Their Own Schoolwork, Even If the Work They Turn In Is Mediocre

THE RULE USED TO BE:
Children are expected to do well, but parents don't do homework.

Our parents were not very involved in school projects. Usually they only came to school on parents' night and open school days, or worse, if there was a problem. (Boy, were you in trouble.) Parents were more concerned with making a living; they did not obsess over their kids' science projects. Our parents were more likely to let us fend for ourselves. Unfortunately, their distance from their children's daily activities meant that they missed the opportunity to bond with their children.

THE RULE BECAME:

Parents overinvolve themselves and do whatever is necessary for the child to get an A.

Collaborative work certainly helps build relationships. But how far should parents go in support of their children? Setting aside time to review your child's homework assignments and checking the completed work encourages children to make schoolwork and academic mastery a priority, but often parents go too far.

The push for academic success begins early. As one preschool teacher laments, "If their child isn't 'reading ready' at three, parents are worried. They tell me, 'My child needs to have an academic edge.'" Today's parents are often very intense.

My friend Jane was having a bad day. A freelance fabric designer, she had a deadline for a major linen manufacturer. However, instead of working at her easel, she was frantically driving around Brooklyn scouring libraries and bookstores. Her nine-year-old daughter, Ashley, had to write a report on famous African-American women, and the shelves at the local branch library turned up bare of helpful resource material. But by the time Ashley arrived home from school that day, she found that her desk was covered with books, including one rather expensive reference book that her mother, acting as her research fairy godmother, had purchased in desperation. Furthermore, Jane sat next to Ashley until the report was finished. Ashley was rewarded with an A that she didn't exactly earn on her own. Unfortunately, Jane missed her deadline and failed *her* assignment.

Like Jane, parents today often go overboard in "helping" their children. They get caught up in showing their child the right way to complete an assignment and stop just short of doing it for them. Backed by computers, Internet technology, and extra cash, we help our children turn out impressive projects that don't accurately represent what the child has learned. Rather, these projects often show the lengths to which Mom or Dad will go to ensure their child's success. Teachers have seen rain forests with actual rain and miniature theater models with working lights.

The problem is that too many parents overidentify with their children. One librarian has grown accustomed to parents coming in alone for materials for a child's project. It was a relief to see a father with his son ask for books on plants that eat animals. So the librarian was taken aback when, after handing the child a book on Venus's-flytraps, the father admonished her, "*I* asked for the books, please respond to *me*."

We often think our child's performance reflects on our own and is a measurement of who we are as parents. It's easier for parents to *do* the child's work than accept mediocre grades or work with the child to improve his mastery of certain knowledge or skills. Such a parent will clean up a child's imperfect homework rather than take the time and effort to review the work with the child and then have the child do it.

Parents and teachers alike may put more emphasis on earning high grades and prizes than they do on individualized learning and academic mastery. Good grades make everyone look good. Many teachers buy into the idea that winning contests is important because it reflects well on their classroom, and the school to the outside world. (If a school has racked up science fair wins with exploding volcanoes created by parents, it typically wants to continue its winning streak.) Before you realize it, parental labor on a project sets the standard.

The Damage

❀ Understand that the more work you do for your kids, the more they come to expect: "If you had helped me better with my math, I wouldn't have failed." Or, "Mom, don't forget to go to the library for me today."

❀ If you do their work for them, they won't be able to duplicate it and will resent you for the help they have come to rely on. Preteens and teens, who are desperately trying to separate from their parents, very often resent close parental help and will strike out at their parents.

HERE'S WHAT WORKS:
Let your kids do their own work, even if what they turn in is mediocre.

When her son showed her his finished report on Christopher Columbus, Marge had to fight the editor in her who desperately wanted to blue pencil the line: "Columbus would of gone sailing sooner, but it took a lot of time to raise the loot." Marge later discovered that many parents routinely type their children's third-grade reports on computers equipped with spelling and grammar checkers. Her computer "would of" loved her son Mark's report. As it turned out, Mark's teacher rewarded the paper with a good grade and corrected his grammar errors so he could learn from them. As the teacher told Marge in a parent-teacher conference, "Don't worry, I can always tell when a parent has done most of the work. It was clear that Mark did this one all by himself."

Decide in advance how much help you will give and stick to it. This will not be easy, particularly when you know that other parents are guided by the principle that they can't do enough.

※ Parents need to be helpful and supportive without being intrusive and eventually unhelpful to their children's education. Teachers today often have no idea what their students really know. Put another way: when Ashley received an A, just whose grade was that anyway?

※ If you have a conscientious kid who is having trouble with a book report or project, you can offer assistance. But if there's a pattern of eleventh-hour trouble, you need to work with your child to develop organizational and planning skills so it doesn't happen again. Help your child break down his assignments into manageable segments: "When do you need to read the first chapter?" "When do you need the first draft?"

※ Let children experience less-than-perfect work. Parents need to understand that it's part of the development of character, strength, and coping skills to learn how to *deserve* an A. It's how kids figure out how to make appropriate choices and set priorities.

※ Be careful how you reward grades. If you make a very big deal for every A the child gets, then you can't be surprised if they enlist your help just to earn it. If your child gets an 83 on an important exam, make sure your first response isn't "How come it wasn't a 90?" It is OK, however, for you to ask her if she thinks a different approach might have earned her a better grade.

We have a society so obsessed with winning that Nike ran this ad after the Olympics: "You don't win silver, you lose gold." We must make sure our kids don't think they fail by not always being golden. Kids who get hooked into every piece of work being perfect are often very hard on themselves. They are the ones who come into doctor's offices literally pulling their hair out or suffering with so-called adult diseases like ulcers and eating disorders.

After all, getting an occasional C can spur your kids on to better study habits. People don't necessarily learn from perfect records of achievement.

✳ **13** ✳

Don't Automatically Take Your Child's Side Against the Teacher

THE RULE USED TO BE:
The teacher is always right.

In the past, the teacher was almost like another parent on the family team. As a result, parents trusted the teacher implicitly as an arbiter in disciplinary matters. Nonetheless, children often felt betrayed when parents automatically accepted the teacher's report. ("You weren't there—how do you know what happened?") Sometimes there were honest misunderstandings, as well as the occasional false accusation. But when parents never took the side of their child and always united with the teacher, this reinforced the lesson that adults are automatically always right, even when they were wrong. Consequently, the child gave up or was bullied into submission.

Furthermore, teachers from the old school tended to be punitive and rarely took into account the varied developmental needs of children. For example, learning disabilities were not well understood. As a result, kids were often categorized by crude labels—either dumb or smart, lazy or industrious. Children tended to live up to or down to the teacher's expectations. So if a child was ever tagged a "troublemaker," for example, it might stick with him all through school.

THE RULE BECAME:
The teacher just doesn't know my child.
My child must be right.

In the turbulent late '60s, teachers, lumped together with *all* authority figures and everyone else over thirty, fell from grace. Their alliance with parents broke down.

The legacy of the '60s is still with us today. Many teachers say that when a note is sent home, parents blame the messenger. Some parents even bad-mouth the teacher in front of the child, which gives the child further license to misbehave.

Parents often become defensive the moment their child is criticized. It's as if the parent feels that his kid is so perfect that the teacher must be talking about someone else. Or they don't like receiving the news that their parenting hasn't produced the desired results. Teachers sometimes react by retreating from giving feedback; they are writing and sending home fewer notes.

One teacher reports, "Typically when I tell a parent something is wrong they come up with excuses for their kid. I'll say, 'Johnny hit Bill on the head with a block.' The response is, 'Oh, Johnny had a bad morning. He didn't get breakfast . . .' or 'Since we had the new baby he's been upset.' But the bottom line is that he hit Bill."

In fact, parents are more likely to confront the *school* for not "doing its job" rather than holding the child responsible. "If a child instigates a food fight and is called a bully," explains a guidance counselor, "the parent wants to know why there weren't more guards in the lunchroom. There is a sense that schools are supposed to provide a perfect environment so the child won't have any problems." Psychologist Ken Condrell offers another good example of a bad parental response: "Mom came to see me because her young son was aggressive and hit other children. The school had advised the mother to get counseling for her son. Her response was to decide that her son must be allergic to the air in school and that was why he was acting nasty. Her child never improved because he was never held responsible for his behavior." Condrell surmises that this boy is still a bully, though now he may be a bully taking allergy pills.

HERE'S WHAT WORKS:
Don't automatically take your child's side against the teacher.

Most of the time teachers have valuable insights because they have an opportunity to observe your child as you never do. Sooner or later you will hear criticism about your child. (He has a short attention span; she is shy; he doesn't turn assignments in on time; she is always being picked on or maybe she is the one doing the picking; he is lagging behind in reading.) Remember, school is your child's home away from home. The teacher is in a unique position to comment on your child's emotional, social, and academic development.

If a teacher does send a note home, or contacts you, realize he is taking his job seriously. The teacher is really doing you a favor by bringing some problem to your attention.

※ Take the note seriously, but don't blow up. Be sure to tell your child that you appreciate the fact that he brought you the note. Get your child's account of the situation.

※ Although your first instinct may be to protect or defend your child, put that feeling on hold and arrange to speak to the teacher. What's important is getting to the bottom of the problem.

※ Don't approach a teacher conference with the assumption that the teacher will blame *you* for your child's behavior. The teacher is equally worried she will be blamed. Everyone is a little defensive when something goes wrong on their watch.

※ Call first and arrange to meet with the teacher by appointment. One kindergarten teacher complains that parents often just show up after she notifies them of some problem: "The parent would be at my door first thing in the morning expecting that I could have a conference about their child while I was in the midst of welcoming the other children."

※ Come in to the teacher conference with an open mind. Start by setting a good tone and say, "Tell me what is going well in school and what isn't, so we can work together." Make sure you leave the session with some specific strategies. (Maybe your child needs tutoring in a particular subject during lunch.)

❋ Hold your child accountable for unacceptable behavior. If he doesn't finish his homework on time, you might take away TV privileges until his work is completed. Or you might make up a behavior report card. (Four typical behaviors that might be included are: completes classroom assignments; follows class rules; cooperates with teachers; cooperates with classmates.) The child is required to bring the report card to school, and at the end of each school day the teacher grades the child + or − in each category. You can then either reward the child or take away privileges depending on how well he is doing.

Although we know that teachers aren't always right, any parent should take complaints seriously enough to do her own mini-investigation. Many of the skills your child needs to do well in school are those she will need later on to function in "real" life. So take criticism to heart and figure out how you and the school can be partners in supporting your child's development of better behavior and study habits.

14

Families Are Not Democracies

THE RULE USED TO BE:
Families are run by dictators, and the dictator is usually Dad.

Daddy was the ruler; his home was HIS castle, after all. Even if sometimes he was a benevolent despot, his word was law, and his orders were to be obeyed without question or complaint. (Just look at the TV titles of the '50s and '60s: *Father Knows Best* and *Make Room for Daddy.*) In general, dictators inspire fear in their subjects and pay little respect to individuals and their needs. With the words "Because I'm the father—that's just the way it is" Dad slammed the door on future discussions. As a result, children were slow to develop a sense of themselves as independent agents.

THE RULE BECAME:
The family should be run as a democracy.

The patriarchal dictatorship was toppled and replaced by the model of the family as a democracy with all members having equal votes.

A major principle of the child-centered parenting movement, which gained influence in the '60s and '70s, is that it is not good for children if parents act like their bosses. Bossing children is critiqued as a put-down that ends up harming their self-esteem. Parents give children reasons for everything they do, even when they set limits. (Explaining to children *why* you set limits may sound reasonable, but they will use the occasion to argue and debate with you. After all, if they don't like your limits, why should they be satisfied with your explanation?)

Parents find themselves forever negotiating with uncompromising young children. The end result is that parents watch as their authority is totally diminished at home. Households of argumentative children proliferate. For example, one seven-year-old boy was outraged that his parents had invited another couple and child for dinner. "But you didn't consult *me*," he protested.

Dr. Ken Condrell, author of *Wimpy Parents: From Toddler to Teen, How Not to Raise a Brat*, observes the result of parental insecurity: "Children today show less respect, are more demanding, and slower to cooperate. Too many parents feel frustrated in getting children to listen, behave, help around the house. Whenever I give talks, I ask the parents in the audience to raise their hands if they are frustrated with the way they argue with their kids. An embarrassed chuckle ripples through the room as hands shoot up."

The problem with being a friend or equal to your child is that friends can't make rules for each other. This generation of moms and dads seems to be afraid of asserting their right to be parental.

HERE'S WHAT WORKS:
Families are not democracies.

Parents need to understand the natural evolution children make from "being the boss" to needing to be bossed. "At around twelve to fifteen months of age, kids start to oppose their parents," explains a pediatrician. "I tell parents that I want them to play along with the kid up until age three. Let the kid express a strong will. So if your child points to a chair and says to you, 'You sit,' I say, go ahead and respond, 'Aye, aye, Captain.' And sit. As long as you do it with humor you are helping to build your child's self-esteem." Parents seldom have problems coping with this imperial period. It's the *next* stage, the dethroning, which is more difficult. Problems arise when parents have to start setting limits and nudging their children off the throne. Parents have trouble taking back the reins. In too many families, the dictator is the *child.*

Consider this scenario: Let's say the family is going out to dinner. You and your husband want to go to an Italian restaurant, but your child begs, "Please, can we have Mexican food?" Maybe you don't really care so you say, "Sure, OK." But if you give in so easily all the time, you end up with a child who feels he is entitled to call the shots. So even if you don't have a preference, you should sometimes go to the Italian restaurant anyway, just because you want your children to know that *you* make the decisions.

✻ It's time to bring back the previously politically incorrect phrase "Because I say so." Sometimes the best answer to a child's endless questions about why they have to do something is simply "Because I say so." This phrase shouldn't be said in anger or exasperation but simply as a matter of fact. If you find this declaration just too reminiscent of your own parents' laying down the law, you can substitute "Because that's the rule in this house." This response works for any situation from "It's time for bed" to "We go to church on Sunday." "Because that's the rule in this house" lets children know that this is the way it *will* be and should eliminate endless discussions.

✻ Give kids only one reason for any of your decisions. For example, if you are turning down your child's request to ride his bike at night, say, "It's not safe," or "You are not old enough," or "I'm not comfortable with that." Period.

✻ Never argue with a child. A teacher warns, "It's like rolling loaded dice. The house, or in this case the kids, always win. If you find yourself in an argument with your child anyway, take the nearest exit as quickly as you can. The argument itself is the means your child will use to wear you down." This teacher gives advice based on years of experience in the trenches: "Avoid using too many words and convey with your body language that the battle is over and you are the victor."

✻ Let your kids know that some issues are open to discussion but others are not. Parents just have to get tough about what's important to them. The following parent drew his own line in the family sand about holidays: "Our family has a tradition that Christmas should be spent at home. Our kids, particularly the teens, don't always want to spend the holidays with us. We say, in no uncertain terms, 'While your grandfather is alive, you will all stay home for Christmas. No questions. You can bring a girlfriend or a boyfriend.' " For another parent it is that all of her children must attend Hebrew school until they are thirteen and then it is each child's decision whether to continue. Each parent can develop their own list of rules that can't be broken.

All family members may be equal in theory, but never forget that parents are more equal than children when it comes to authority. You are running a family, not a small country. There is no need to install a democracy in your house.

15

No Parent Always Knows Best— There Is No Need to Be Perfect

THE RULE USED TO BE:
Father knows best.

If father knew best, what about mom? The old-time perspective on parental authority was at best contradictory; at worst, it wasn't even true. There was a lot of role playing in our parents' homes. Though Mom scurried and deferred to Dad, she was often only making it look as if Dad knew best. What's more, both parents rarely admitted it when one of them did make mistakes.

THE RULE BECAME:
The parenting experts know best.

In the quest to get parenting down "right," the power and influence shifted from the all-knowing Dad to the author of the latest parenting book.

Today, parents rarely trust their own instincts. They rely on others to tell them how to parent. One mother still shudders when she discusses her former days of parenting by the book. She was wrestling with her toddler's getting up in the night, and she read a popular book, *Crying Baby; Sleepless Nights,* which advocated not coming into the room when your child cries at night. "The advice didn't feel right, but I followed it anyway," she confesses. "But then I was really proud of myself because he did eventually stop crying." When she went in to check, Jack was asleep all right, but lying in a big pool of his own vomit. Now this mom follows only the advice that feels right and is consistent with her own views of parenting. (So when Jack was a little older and started coming into her bedroom at night, she put a sleeping bag next to her bed. She told her son, "If you insist on coming in, then just lay down on this sleeping bag so Dad and I won't be disturbed." Within a short period Jack and his sleeping bag disappeared back into his room.)

Today's mom often tries too hard. "A woman accustomed to bringing consummate energy to her job now transfers that into childrearing," observes one pediatrician. "Moms bring a certain intensity and obsession for perfection. They worry way too much about failing their child in any way."

To calm their insecurity, parents need a lot of approval and affirmation that they measure up as parents. As a mother of four and grandmother of six observes, "I never called *my* mother up to see how I was doing as a mother. Both my son and my daughter-in-law always call me the day after I visit with dozens of questions: 'Isn't Jason really smart?' 'Doesn't he have a terrific vocabulary?' 'Did you notice the way Jennifer is drinking out of a cup already?' " As this woman observes, "They seem to need me to approve of every single thing they do."

HERE'S WHAT WORKS:
No parent always knows best.
There's no need to be perfect.

"Many parents have unrealistic standards about being a parent," says Dr. Judi Craig, author of *Parents on the Spot!* "It's as if they took a pledge: 'I shall always be consistent, fair, calm, reasonable, forgiving, available, cheerful, understanding, positive, and totally loving. Above all, I will never lose it with my child.' " This is a pledge you can't easily live up to, so don't take it in the first place.

❋ Trying to be perfect is the worst thing you can do to your child. Perfect parents pay a high price in exhaustion for their perfectionism and give their kids a model they can't live up to. Trying to be perfect puts great stress on parents and minimizes their enjoyment of their family-focused time.

❋ Perfection is only an illusion. It doesn't exist. Kay Willis, mother of ten, cheerfully explains, "There is no state of perfection on the map. If you continually go looking for it you may miss the really good stuff."

❋ Relax: you can't "win" all the time, anyway. As an example, a mother cites how the family dealt with buying presents at Christmas. "We always put a lot of effort into gifts: we had categories—one gift should be to hug, one to read, something musical, and one WOW gift." Yet what do her grown children recall? This mother laughs, "Each one still remembers what they always wanted and *didn't* get."

✳ When your imperfections as a parent inevitably show, don't forget the value of apologizing. If you were short-tempered or made a misguided snap judgment, admit to it. If you hurt your child's feelings unintentionally, an "I'm sorry, I was insensitive," or "I wasn't thinking" is good. Kids should know you are capable of making mistakes. And remember it is just as important to apologize to a four-year-old as it is to a twelve-year-old.

My friend Pam, a busy accountant, was interrupted at 3:10 one afternoon by her receptionist, who asked, "Will you accept a collect call from Tim?" Tim was her eight-year-old son. He was standing on the street near school with no money waiting for his mom to meet him so they could go clothes shopping. Mom had simply lost track of time. The best of us sometimes goof, take the wrong path, misread the signs.

Over time *you* are bound to occasionally mess up and make a couple of less than ideal decisions. You may start out by declaring, "In my house I will never plop my kids in front of the TV or let them eat cookies." Then your kids are fussy and you put them in front of the TV and actually say, "Stop fussing and I'll give you a cookie." My son, now sixteen, delights in reminding me that I once slightly overdosed him on cough medicine. As he recalls, "Remember the time in preschool when I fell asleep in my cupcake and you had to come and get me?"

Try and correct your mistakes on the spot, and then forgive yourself. Children don't need perfect parents, they need loving ones.

❋ 16 ❋

Teach Respect for Others

THE RULE USED TO BE:
Respect adults without question.

Just as brides once routinely promised to love, honor, and obey their husbands, children were once trained to obey *all* adults. But always following the dictates of authority figures without question would sometimes yield unpleasant consequences.

I still vividly recall a fire drill when I was in the third grade. My teacher had sternly warned us, "Do *not* speak or move out of line, no matter what." I was forced to join hands with a sweaty little boy and leave the classroom. Suddenly my new gold pinkie ring, the one with the birthstone given to me for my ninth birthday, slipped off my finger. I tried to inch my way over to where the ring had fallen, but my partner sharply pulled me back. When we were finally let back into the building after the all-clear signal, I raised my hand and got permission to go look for the ring, but of course it wasn't there. The teacher understood why I hadn't broken out of the line, but my parents were not so understanding. They kept asking me incredulously, "How could you just leave the ring lying there?" Answer: I was being a good obedient girl, a true product of the '50s.

MORE RECENTLY THE RULE BECAME:
All children should feel free to question authority.

In our more permissive age, parents go out of their way to make sure their children won't be little Stepford kids who follow authority blindly. This is a common baby-boomer reaction to the uptight, Cold War '50s of our childhood.

America's cultural revolution of the late '60s and '70s left us skeptical of all institutions, from the Catholic Church to the presidency. Now popular characters on TV blatantly show how to be disrespectful and talk back to adults, validated by an accompanying laugh track. (Think Beavis and Butt-Head yet again, or any of the smart-mouthed sitcom kids.)

As a result, there's a measurable decline in respect for adult authority. In the old days, for example, police officers were naturally looked up to, even feared. Now if two teens see a cop on the street they are as likely to mutter "Oink, oink" as to show respect.

Child psychologist Ken Condrell reports that he hears story after story of disrespect from teachers, parents, grandparents. "I went to talk to a fifth-grade class," says the psychologist. "Not only did they seem indifferent to me as an authority figure, one kid even

said, 'What right do YOU have to tell me what to do?' "
Condrell recently witnessed an eight-year-old boy
swear at his teacher on the grounds of a Catholic school,
and he is even being asked to consult at day care cen-
ters, where children as young as two are described as
out of control.

HERE'S WHAT WORKS:
Teach respect for others.

An elementary school principal recalls that in a recent
conference with a parent and child, he told the boy, "You
have to listen to your father." The child said, "And he
has to listen to me. Right?" Wrong. The father had *never*
made it clear to his son that he, as a parent, was the boss
(see chapter 14, Families Are Not Democracies). Children
need to begin to respect others by first learning to respect
their parents.

All adults are not automatically in the right, but parents make a big mistake if they raise children who don't
start their engagement with authority figures with a certain amount of courtesy. As children mature they can
learn that there are appropriate times to challenge authority, and then with tact and due respect.

※ Understand that children learn from you. How you
   deal with the other adults in their lives will go a long
   way toward establishing whether your child relates to
   them appropriately. Parents often talk about authority
   figures in front of their children in very negative ways.
   ("That miserable so-and-so, who does he think he is
   not to choose you for the squad?") You can't expect

children to be respectful if they hear disrespect from you. Just as you shouldn't be negative, make sure you point out instances where someone is especially deserving of respect. ("I really respect your basketball coach. He lets all the kids get a turn. Most of the coaches bench the poorer players, but your coach never does that.")

※ Reinforce the idea of showing respect to adults. Teach children that if a person is in a position of authority, they do have to listen to him or her. You can also explain, "If you need to challenge an authority figure tell me, and we will decide how to handle it." (Maybe a coach is repeatedly unfair, or a teacher accused your child of something he didn't do.)

※ Make sure your children understand they need to respect people they may not like. Obviously children will not get along with every adult they come in contact with. One mother of four explains how she deals periodically with the inevitable difficult teacher. As she says, "There's always a teacher one of my kids doesn't like. Usually they think the teacher is too strict and gives too much homework. I never rush up to school and say, 'Be nicer to my kid.' " Instead, this mother talks to the child and points out, "You have to learn how to adjust to different adults in your life. Not all teachers are going to be like Mommy." But bottom line, says this mom: "While you are in her class, you will show her respect."

Make sure your children respect *you* as an authority figure. It should be clear to them that there are rules that have to be followed and consequences when they are not.

Don't let your children ever abuse or mistreat you. You can also point out to older kids how important respect is to them: the worst thing a teen can do to another is "dis" him.

✳ **17** ✳

It's OK for Your Kids to Fear You a Little

THE RULE USED TO BE:
Kids should always fear their parents.

We feared our parents and acknowledged their power over us. "When I was growing up in New Jersey back in the '40s—you know, when dinosaurs roamed the earth," jokes one dad, "my brothers and I used to pummel each other until we got bloody teeth. As soon as my father's car pulled into the garage, we would just stop. We knew if we were still out of order by the time he reached the top of the stairs, some unknown horror would befall us. We also knew Dad loved us and was not going to abuse us, but we knew not to test him. My brothers and I were in awe of Dad and had an appropriate degree of fear for *all* other adults we knew." (The brothers were equally grim if Mom caught them misbehaving; she would promptly report them to Dad.)

THE RULE BECAME:
Parents almost fear their kids.

Parents do not want to loom as scary authority figures the way our parents did. We are so hypersensitive to power's potential abuse that we are loathe to leverage any power as parents, however responsibly we act. We are afraid of becoming our parents at their worst. As a mother of four admits, "I used to be terrified of my mother, who screamed a lot. I don't want my kids to feel like that. It's not easy making sure they know what line not to cross and having them still like me."

As we've seen, too many parents want their children to be their best buddy, so they stop being their parent. The balance of power between parents and children in today's families has shifted so dramatically that parents are often the ones asking their children for permission and begging their pardon. Remember Jean, the mom who lets her child hit her? ("Oh, he only does that if I talk to another adult.") By refusing to correct his abusive behavior, she is condoning his actions and accepting them, an indication that she fears her son instead of the other way around.

It's actually scary for children to boss parents around. "Never forget," one parent observes, "the child is supposed to look to the parent as a protector." As we've seen, kids need parents to set boundaries and borders to their lives. Children may act like they don't want you to be the boss, but that doesn't mean they are prepared to be the boss. (There are many popular movies built around the concept of children being temporarily trapped inside adult bodies: think *Big* or *Freaky Friday*, where the child always winds up uncomfortable in a grown-up world with power he can't handle.) Children need to experience small doses of power just as they learned to experience small doses of frustration.

HERE'S WHAT WORKS:
It's OK for your kids to fear you a little.

Children need to acknowledge that their parents can affect their quality of life; in other words, parents can punish them. "If you are doing a good job," says a child psychologist, "your child should occasionally say, 'I hate you.' " With respect comes a little fear.

❋ Children should be apprehensive not that their parents will hurt them but that they could lose privileges if they displease them. Parents worry that they come on too strong and will damage their kids, but more often they come on too weak.

❋ You never want to frighten your child with the threat of abandonment or rejection. No matter how angry you may be, never say anything like "If you don't stop doing that I'm going to have to send you away." It doesn't matter that you are vague about where the child will go. *You* know you don't really mean it, but a young child does not. A child does not need to be "broken" to learn a lesson, or you will spend a lot of time repairing the relationship.

❋ It's your job as parent to teach your kids what is right and what is wrong. Children should be free of irrational, immobilizing fear, but if they cross a clear behavioral boundary, guilt should tell them "oh-oh." All guilt is not pathological; some is very healthy (see chapter 29, Let Your Kids (Occasionally) Feel Guilty).

❋ Your kids need to know that in your household, parents run the show, make the rules, set consequences for behavior, and follow through. If you've fallen into a wimpy parenting style, put your kids on alert that there is going to be a major shift in power.

Keep in mind that a parent is supposed to be a powerful presence in a child's life. It's OK for your child to seek your approval and to be fearful when she breaks the rules. On the other hand, make sure that your kids know that you love them. Children who both love and fear their parents are strongly motivated to accept parental guidance.

※ **18** ※

Both the Quantity and Quality of the Time You Spend with Your Children Matter

THE RULE USED TO BE:
Parents rarely monitor the amount of time they spend with their kids.

Parents didn't go out of their way to spend special time with their children. The family gathered for daily meals and occasions that were uniformly observed: Sunday dinner, worship, and certain holidays. Parents who scheduled one-on-one time with individual kids, either to play board games or to have a heart-to-heart talk, were unusually attentive and conscientious.

THE RULE BECAME:
"Quality time" is what matters.

In the 1970s, when women were heading into the paid workforce in unprecedented numbers, they craved reassurance that it was OK to have both a job and a family. Of course it's OK, but it's not an easy juggling act. Someone, probably an exhausted working parent struggling with guilt, came up with the idea of quality versus quantity time. If parents couldn't spend long hours with their children, they were urged to put extra effort into the time they could be with them. Mothers and fathers found themselves working hard to create idyllic family occasions.

But the trade-off isn't that easy. The mother of six children notes, "Quality time is often a tired mother trying to do crafts with a cranky child or a woman pulling out flash cards while she stirs pasta. It's forced." Often a child would really be happier just sitting and playing with her Legos.

Too many parents have been lulled into thinking parenting can be scheduled into neat fifteen-minute daily appointments. One wife complains about her husband: "Bob used to say, I believe in QTWD. I finally said, 'What is QTWD?' He explained that was 'quality time with Daddy.' That's what he called the fifteen minutes he spent with the boys after his evening martini." But as this mom notes, "Unfortunately QTWD doesn't give kids the idea that they are any more important than any other thing on his daily to-do list" (especially when the fifteen minutes is typically spent watching TV or playing video games together, and then Dad moves on to his next activity).

HERE'S WHAT WORKS:
Both the quantity and quality of the time you spend with your children matter.

It's necessary to rethink the concept of "quality time" to include any time spent with your children. Just being in

the same room with Mommy or Daddy has quality to it.
Be there for your kids as a sitting target: Let the kids find
you, and the quantity of encounters will quickly add up.

✳ Kids do need a *quantity* of time with their parents. Time
spent together can be "special" no matter what you are
doing. So sit your toddler on the dryer while you fold
clothes. As one parent says; "Just laying around with
the paper on Sunday letting the kids make breakfast if
they want to—that's much better than saying, 'On Sunday between two and four we're going to get all
dressed up and go to the museum to see the Michelan-
gelo exhibit.' "

One recent study said toddlers need at least two
hours a day of parental contact. A parent could do that
from 4–6 P.M., but that doesn't fit a toddler's limited
attention span. A better solution is for a parent to give
two minutes a day—sixty times.

✳ On the other hand, it's nice if some of your time with
each child can be special. So on occasion take a child
to lunch or a movie, or just read with him on your lap,
and don't forget to play Scrabble with the child who
loves word games. Think like our grandparents did:
"Treat your family like company and your company
like family." (And maybe it's not a bad idea to turn
back to the extended family and enlist grandparents
and other relatives who are available, so children can
spend more time with people who adore them.)

One father explains how he and his family include
both quantity and quality time every day: "The four of
us sit down and have dinner together almost every night.
We're laughing and telling jokes and teasing. We really

do ask what happened in school; they ask what happened with us. Sometimes we get in deep philosophical discussions and sometimes we don't." As he sums up how he and his wife feel: "We don't use the term 'quality' time. Spending time with the kids is the most important thing to us." If you invite your children to be part of your life, they will happily join you.

✳ **19** ✳

Don't Treat Boys and Girls Exactly the Same, but Keep Their Options Open

IT USED TO BE:
Boys and girls are different and need to be treated differently.

In the old days boys and girls practically came with pink or blue manuals proclaiming what they were made of: "sugar and spice and everything nice" for girls, and "snips and snails, and puppy-dog tails" for boys. Parents treated their sons and daughters differently because that was nature's blueprint: believing that there were specific ways boys and girls should behave, they molded their children to follow those patterns.

It was just assumed that boys were naturally aggressive and should be encouraged to be athletic and dominant; girls were programmed to be submissive and to grow up to be just like their moms.

The problem with making sure boys and girls were

brought up according to separate programs was that the programs were *not* quite equal. Girls were pretty much second-class citizens with strict ceilings placed on their aspirations.

THE RULE BECAME:
Treat boys and girls exactly the same.

Influenced by the women's movement that emerged in the 1970s, psychologists and child-rearing experts began to focus on how rigidly prescribed sex roles kept children from growing up healthy and free. As the '70s turned into the '80s, we threw out the "sugar and spice" model of female character, realizing instead that girls don't always need to be so nice. In fact, being nice all of the time could be a liability in the real world.

Somehow the notion that girls should be able to do anything got translated into the idea that boys and girls are just the same. Many parents became committed to raising little nonsexists. Out went the blue and pink tell-tale clothes; in came unisex names like Morgan and Taylor. Believing that nurture creates behavioral differences, parents assume they can get more assertive girls if they just give them trucks and Erector sets and more loving boys if they present them with dolls.

Nonetheless, even parents who are committed to being politically correct often aren't prepared for the reality of their own feelings and reactions to a world of blended genders. As one mother admits, "When I first had my daughter I didn't dress her up frilly or in pink, and this was a problem because she was one of those completely *bald* little kids, and people always thought she was a boy.

She had no hair until she was a year-and-a-half. I never thought this would bother me, but it really did when people called her a boy. But *she* didn't know or care."

Sometimes the results of minimizing gender differences are a lot more confusing than just having a stranger identifying your child by the wrong sex. One mother explains how she and her husband carefully substituted "she" for "he" when they read to their daughter Jessy, and how they used female pronouns to refer to Jessy's stuffed animals: "But now at four, Jessy seems to be confused about gender pronouns altogether. She sometimes refers to her father as 'her.' "

"It's been my experience," observes a pediatrician "that most parents are really not comfortable with a neutral gender." The reality of raising children keeps slapping you in the face with gender specifics. For example, a little girl would harbor a desire for makeup and would try to put lipstick on with a red crayon. And a little boy would "roar" and tumble. "Is it all right for my child to do that?" worried parents ask their pediatricians. One doctor's answer: "What you want are children who like who they are and who feel they have options." Blurring all gender lines didn't create happier, healthier children.

HERE'S WHAT WORKS:
Don't treat boys and girls exactly the same, but keep their options open.

Psychologists now understand that girls and boys are just "hard-wired" differently by the biochemistry of gender. From the get-go there is an intrinsic difference between boys and girls. Just ask parents.

As one father admits almost reluctantly, "I thought it was all socialization, but what I've seen and observed is that even as infants, girls and boys seem to have different traits. The girls are calmer and more apt to do little loving things like taking care of their toys and combing their dolls' hair, while the boys are more apt to destroy things, be rambunctious, and get in trouble. My daughter is very loving and makes sure all her dolls are tucked in on the couch. We didn't buy into the fact that boys and girls were different. But they are."

This is echoed by a divorced mother raising two sons who has observed that they are very "male" even though they don't spend much time with their father. She says, "As the mother of two sons who grew up with sisters I'm learning as I go along. I was brought up at the time when we talked about there not being much difference between boys and girls—but clearly there is a sort of boy energy that is more aggressive. And they are always having races with vehicles and playing with tools. When boys have a disagreement they just give the other one a kick and they are done with it. Girls don't do that; they are more complex and emotional. From what I can see, if I had a girl, there would be different parenting."

❋ Expect and accept differences in your children. Understand that just as you shouldn't treat *all* girls the same because of individual differences, neither should you treat boys and girls exactly the same. Maybe one daughter loves competitive team sports, while the other daughter is into chess, cello, and drawing. The mother of three sons describes how they differ from each other: "Nathaniel, the oldest, is the artist who sits and draws animals, Jonah is a natural musician, and Ben is a real 'techie'—he loves math, science, and devours science fiction.''

✳ "Viva la difference.'' That's the advice of Kay Willis, founder of the national organization Mothers Matter, and the mother of ten children—six girls followed by four boys. Her house was a living textbook on gender differences. She says, ''I tried to treat my kids all the same for a while. Ben was the first son after six girls. He never touched his sisters' toys, but he did take their carriage, turn it upside down, and spin the wheels. That was a major clue.'' Yet Willis notes that all six of her daughters watched and read sports with their dad. (As a result, all the girls know sports as well as most men, and one daughter is a sports producer for a morning news show.)

✳ Don't try to undo what Mother Nature has programmed. So don't push cooking lessons on boys *unless* the boy wants it. It's OK, once again, for little girls to play dress up and for boys to find their own more energetic activities. A mother of both a son and daughter observes the *benefits* of today's more realistic view of raising the sexes. "My daughter Maggie plays ice hockey, soccer, and lacrosse, but she also has piles of hairdo magazines for her friends to go through. The neat thing is that today girls can have it all. And boys like my son are allowed to show their sensitive and nurturing side.''

✳ Be flexible when it comes to toys. There are a whole range of toys appropriate for either a boy *or* a girl: yo-yos, Tickle Me Elmos, puzzles, and paint sets, to name just a few. But in addition, it's OK to give girls dolls and boys blocks and trucks if they want them. A mother of three says, "I am totally convinced that boys and girls have an innate, inborn chemical attraction to different kinds of toys. I swear there is a truck gene. I'm not saying that there aren't girls who have it, but mostly boys do. Boys can make truck noises that no girl child can make." The bottom line is that kids should be able to play with the toys *they* choose, and feel passionate about. Take your kids to a toy store, where there are plenty of choices, and watch what they pick up. And you can always make suggestions: offer your son a male Cabbage Patch doll, if he wants one, to go along with his sleek new Batmobile; and your daughter might like a truck to ride her new doll around in.

Make sure your boys have plenty of stuffed animals to hug and cuddle. (The divorced mother of sons notes that her older son, eight, never goes anywhere without his favorite whale tucked under his arm.) And let your girls literally shoot for the sky. Encourage girls to be assertive and make sure they have a wide variety of career choices and options. The bottom line is to allow our sons and daughters to pass through wider doors without restrictive labels. As Kay Willis says, "All my children were taught that anything was possible for them." There is something to be said for supporting and being proud of having a son or daughter: "I'm so glad you are my little girl." Or, "I treasure my son." We should be raising a generation free to be whatever they are.

✳ 20 ✳

Read to Your Children What You Both Enjoy

THE RULE USED TO BE:
It's OK to read children everything.

Our parents generally read us anything available in the children's section of the library or bookstore without any thought to the story's political implications. We innocently enjoyed yarns about cowboys and Indians, classic fairy tales, mysteries like Nancy Drew for girls and the Hardy Boys for, well, boys. Actually, many of these narratives were rather sweet, though they usually featured characters who did not reflect our lives. We were lulled to sleep with inspiring and instructive tales starring little engines that could or even garbage trucks named Katie. The big test was not whether a story was "politically correct"—there was no such language—but whether it was a calming and cozy bedtime story.

THE RULE BECAME:
We must always be politically correct.

The current trend is to screen the stories we read to our
children, making sure they are politically correct—that is,
they don't offend anyone. Obviously there is a need for
some sensitivity to cultural differences and pejorative im-
ages. (For example, all step-relatives, particularly step-
mothers and stepsisters, get a bad rap in fairy tales.)

We seem to be living in an ultra-sensitive time, and
many parents are easily confused about where to draw
the politically correct line. Some end up feeling like modern-
day Freuds, reading between the sentences to find hidden
political meanings when children would never see or hear
any. (So children don't think *all* Indians must be "dumb"
because Tiger Lily says "ugh" a lot in *Peter Pan*. And
most girls who read Cinderella won't be permanently un-
assertive and wait around to be rescued by a Prince
Charming.)

A new category of children's books has arisen, written
to reflect the variety of lifestyles and family forms in
which many children live today. Books like *Heather Has
Two Mommies* and those recounting what it's like to be the
child of divorce like *"Where Is My Toothbrush?"* are now
widely available. These new reality-based books have not
replaced standards like *Goodnight Moon* or even *Charlotte's
Web*. Books like *Marvin's Terrible Day* haven't taken the
place of classic favorites.

HERE'S WHAT WORKS:
Read your children whatever you both enjoy.

Parents should resist the temptation to translate all stories into politically correct terms. Again, sensitivity is important, but don't be too paranoid about committing some act of political incorrectness. Kids love to hear the story of Snow White and the seven dwarfs. It's not necessary to retitle it "Snow White and the Seven Vertically Challenged Young Men."

Understand that classic fairy tales have a definite place in children's literature. They provide a good springboard for useful discussions with your kids. The story "Hansel and Gretel" helps children understand, for example, that there are rules you have to follow ("Don't go into the woods") and that there are dangerous people in the world. Although your kids are unlikely to meet up with a wicked witch in a gingerbread house, they will encounter unsavory characters in all guises throughout their lives.

In most of the classics, like "The Three Little Pigs," the story ends just like life, with something good and something bad happening. In this particular tale, someone gets eaten, but someone else gets saved. And there is a valuable lesson to be learned from the enterprising pig who uses bricks to build his house; he's the only one who doesn't turn into lunch. (In some of the *newer* sanitized versions the two pigs who are initially eaten get to magically reappear at the end, when the wolf finally gets his just desserts.)

There's a reason why fairy tales have been popular for so long. Children respond to scary tales (think of the very popular *Goosebumps* series) and can tolerate a whole range of emotions. Bruno Bettelheim reminds us that children, in particular, have a need for fantasy. And some of the classic tales help them handle many of their own often frightening and violent fantasies.

❋ Parents should make the key choices. You decide what is appropriate for your children to read and, as they get older, what they can view. "The way I see it most of the Disney stories are pretty awful," observes a parent of a daughter. "None of the heroines have mothers. I can't think of a one. But we don't exclude Disney from her reading or television diet because she enjoys them so much. We just try to include other stories that have strong heroines. We do go with classic children's literature and just try to balance things out in the end."

❋ You can read your children anything and *editorialize* along the way. As the parent who doesn't like Disney continues, "When I read to my daughter about boy characters I do find myself affirming to her, 'Now girls can do that, too.' " (And when you get to those wicked stepmother stories, give your child real life examples of loving stepfamilies.)

❋ Don't be too quick to send out the PC police! One sheepish dad who watches very little television has a guilty pleasure: "We rarely watch TV. The one program we watch religiously is *The Simpsons*. I think it's the best stuff on TV. Our conversations are full of Simpsons jokes. We talk about the plots, what's funny and why." (And this family routinely gives each other books about the Simpsons as gifts.) Not everyone would give a politically correct thumbs-up to the Simpsons with their resident brat, Bart.

✳ What's important is to *know your child*. Be aware that there are those little children who really love *Lion King* and master the trauma of losing a parent, but then there are those kids who cannot bear the aggression. (Remember, this is just Hamlet played out by African animals, after all.) Listen to your children and your own heart.

Children often enjoy listening to the words of stories and don't interpret them the way adults do. Some tales just magically work time after time. *Every* generation of children has clapped to keep Tinkerbell alive.

✳ **21** ✳

It's Still No Drugs—No Way, No How—But Here's Why

THE RULE USED TO BE:
No drugs. No alcohol. End of story.

In the old days parents expected their children not to stray, not even to sample the so-called forbidden fruit. They simply had a list of no-nos and then went on a search-and-destroy mission for contraband. There was no presumption of privacy. In general kids knew better than to smuggle in any forbidden items such as cigarettes or beer.

But this policy often didn't work. A father, George, describes how it used to be: "Our parents were all in denial. Mom and Dad couldn't imagine what it was like being a teenager, and the temptations we would face. I remember when I admitted to my parents that I smoked pot in high school and later at Harvard, they were totally shocked. And I was just as shocked that they were shocked."

George recalls that parents of that generation reacted by getting angry, maybe even by throwing the offender out of the house, and by continuing to forbid the activity: "It was taboos, and 'How dare you?' and 'No child of mine would do that.' " The problem was that everyone knew a child of someone who was doing just that.

THE RULE BECAME:

Maybe we should talk about this, and YOU can decide what's right.

Most parents would like to just say no, but they are not comfortable with the role of dictator. The more modern way is to say "Let's talk about it." But as much as we encourage talk about issues in general, we don't really want to get into philosophical discussions about the pros and cons of pot. Still, some of us do. We want to trust our kids and to give them the opportunity to choose the right road, but it's often a rocky path to get there.

Some parents get stuck with their own youthful hippie ideals. Remember, *we* are the parents who went to Woodstock. ("OK, Mom," said one son eagerly, "tell me, how many joints did you smoke that weekend?" It's a personal decision, of course, how to answer that question.) In an effort to be realistic and nonjudgmental (the way we wish our parents were), some parents wind up offering the forbidden fruit and then cross their fingers and hope that the child doesn't bite.

When Ally was thirteen, her father asked her if she would like a cigarette. "At first I was astounded," she recalls. "My father explained it this way: I know you are going to want to try, and I would rather you get your first cigarette from me. You should know that this is really a dirty, expensive habit.' The truth was I was torn: On one hand a lot of my friends had started to smoke and I thought it looked glamorous, but on the other I could see for myself what a disgusting habit it was." Ally turned down her father's offer, but she did accept a cigarette when a "glamorous" friend offered one at a party. Ally felt she had her dad's *permission*, although initially she chose to smoke out of his presence. By fifteen she was addicted.

Will knew that his sixteen-year-old son Thomas was experimenting with alcohol, so he decided to deal with it head-on: "I got him a six-pack and we got drunk together. He woke up really sick and with a bad headache. I said, 'Is this your idea of fun?' " Will, a high school chemistry teacher, explains why he chose this route: "Kids can't be lectured. They need to experience things on their own. You can make the experience good or bad. I wanted Thomas to visualize drinking as *bad* from now on."

Even though parents try to sour the fruit, some kids still find it a "sweet" experience. The problem with these strategies is that they often backfire. (Just ask Ally's dad.) Also, the parent becomes too much like the child's confidante or even, in cases like Thomas, a literal drinking buddy.

Some modern parents try to attack the problem intellectually: they tell their kids why they shouldn't do drugs and trust them to listen. A father explains, "We had a lot of conversations about drugs with our daughter especially as she hit junior high school. We specifically talked about drugs that destroy brain cells, because she's so into being smart. We wanted her to believe us when we told her what *we* think is really dangerous—cigarettes, cocaine, and alcohol." The problem is the child heard the message, only too well. She did lay off the drugs that she believed would hurt her academically and picked the ones she felt were less harmful—like pot.

The modern approach clearly doesn't work if your goal is to stop kids from using drugs or alcohol. It is very difficult to simply *talk* sense into a teen.

HERE'S WHAT WORKS:
It's still No. No way, no how. (But here's why.)

Understand that *all children want what they can't have*. It's a given that the more you tell a teenager that something is off limits, the more tempted she is to cross over into the forbidden territory. Parents are going to have to decide how to handle the inevitable time when their teen is interested in "sex, drugs, and rock and roll," not to mention cigarettes and alcohol.

It's time to turn from negotiator to temporary dictator and, yes, just say no. Parents need to firmly stand up to a teen who is unreasonable or who wants to do something that is dangerous and could ultimately harm her. Despite what she initially says, in many cases your teen is actually begging you to say no for her.

But she will need the "no" accompanied by an explanation. You don't want to play the part of a tyrant, as it will leave her feeling like a peon. That's a breeding ground for resentment, which is exactly what you don't need right now.

❋ Make sure your teen has basic information about the legalities of alcohol and drug use. It is illegal. Period. Tell him in detail, for example, what would happen if pot is found stashed in his locker at school, or if he is ever arrested for driving while intoxicated. (However, most parents wisely let their child know that if he is ever in a situation where he has had too much to drink or he is with a driver who has that they will come without question and pick him up. Your child must have an "out" without worrying about your immediate response. The priority, after all, is always your child's safety.)

❋ Point out that the activity could land BOTH of you in legal trouble. When Maryann had a party to celebrate her daughter's "sweet 16," she found empty bottles of some sweet-smelling liquor out on the terrace. Just three weeks earlier, Maryann's neighbor had been fined $600 for kids drinking in her backyard. "Instead of a lecture, I wanted my daughter's friends to know that I didn't want to get fined and have my name on the front of the *Montclair Times.* I said, 'This is the way New Jersey law reads about alcohol and minors. You can't argue with the law. You cannot drink in my backyard.' "

❋ Make sure your teen understands the consequences of breaking the rules. Infractions have to bring very severe and related consequences. Take the car keys away from your teen because he drove with alcohol on his breath, and keep the keys in your control. The punishment might be no use of the car for a month. Again, always try to relate the punishment to the specific crime. If your teen is caught smoking in his room, then for a specific period of time his door stays open until lights out. (One parent, who found cigarette burns in her daughter's blanket, installed a supersensitive smoke alarm system, not as a punishment but as a safety precaution.)

✳ Don't be afraid to confront your teen when you do think he is doing something unsafe—whether the signs are telltale cigarette burns (see above) or beer cans in his trash basket or a roach clip in his sock drawer. Even if he denies the stuff is his, *he* is responsible for what winds up in his room, and he must suffer the consequences. Generally it is not a good idea to just storm your teen's room. "That's not playing fair," says one therapist, who advises, "if you think your kid might be using drugs, say, 'I hope I'm wrong but your eyes are the size of half-dollars and your behavior is strange. I need to be convinced you are not doing drugs. I'd like you to pee in a cup.' " Of course, your child will try to "blow you off," but it's *your* decision how far to go to find out whether or not he's involved with drugs.

✳ Don't bail your teen out when he's in trouble. Dr. Judi Craig, author of *You're Grounded till You're Thirty*, advises, "Don't take the teen off the hook and help him to avoid actual consequences." For example, she says, "Don't be too much of a caretaker. ('Let me help you clean up the vomit and get you some clean sheets.') And don't let him lay blame elsewhere ('I knew those friends of yours were a rotten influence')." True, his friends may be a bad influence, but he's the one who bit into the forbidden fruit. Your child must be allowed to experience the consequences of his alcohol or drug use. If necessary, get professional help.

We can never entirely protect our children from all the forbidden apples out there, but we can wise them up about the potential poison and stay poised to administer antidotes when necessary.

✳ 22 ✳

Don't Fight Every Battle

THE RULE USED TO BE:
Parents rule the roost on all issues.

Parents often took strong stands on every issue from clean plates to clean rooms and just about everything in between. As we've noted, it was the parents' way or no way. They wielded the same decision-making power over toddlers and teens, exhibiting little understanding that adolescence requires a moderated approach.

Psychologist Ken Condrell shares a case history that points out the effect of trying to wield too much control over an adolescent: "Jim was a well-behaved boy on honor roll who was his parents' pride and joy. By sixteen he was a normal teen who wanted to make his own decisions and to spend more time away from home. His parents made a rule that Monday through Sunday Jim was allowed out of the house only twice a week after dinner. He began to date a particular girl. His parents came up with a new rule that he couldn't go out twice in succession with the same girl. He found a job. Now the rule was that Jim had to discuss all of his purchases because his parents were concerned he would throw away his money. Mom routinely searched Jim's room and found *Playboy* magazines. Now his parents declared that his bedroom door must remain open." As Condrell explains, every aspect of Jim's behavior was controlled by his parents. The stage was set for war: "Jim took up the challenge by purchasing a six hundred dollar stereo. In less than twenty-four hours his dad had locked it in the hall closet. Jim found a hacksaw and cut off the doorknob." Once war was declared, the battles never ended, and Jim started to give his parents real reasons to be concerned. He skipped school and began drinking beer for breakfast. It took years to establish a truce and eventually peace. But Jim still carries the emotional and psychic scars of this ballistic period.

THE RULE BECAME:
"Let's All Be Friends."

Parents today want to keep the lines of communication open between themselves and their teens. The name of the game is "flexibility." So, when asked, "Why can't I stay up later?" or "Why do I have to go with you to Grandmas' house? It's boring," parents today think, "Hmm. Let me consider this." Parents frequently react by catering to the teen's many demands or by giving vague, confusing messages. ("Well, I guess it might be OK just this once not to go to Grandma.")

Anxious not to create conflict during this highly reactive time, parents strive to be their kids' "best bud" and fail to let teens know how they really feel about issues.

On one level this is a freeing experience for an adolescent. On another, deeper level, it's frightening. After all, who exactly holds the reins, and will they be pulled in when necessary? Even the wildest of adolescents knows that while he would like to be the master of his own fate, he may not be up to the job.

HERE'S WHAT WORKS:
Don't fight every battle.

Parenting an adolescent is a difficult balancing act. Too much control during this period only leads to real problems. Too little control leaves kids floundering without boundaries. Don't stop setting limits—just be more careful how you use your authority. Teens don't need you to make their every decision for them but rather to guide, encourage, and mentor them. Let your children know that when they come to you, there will be a dialogue and not just a monologue on your part.

As we've seen in the previous chapter, it *is* necessary to stand firm on the safety issues (drugs, alcohol), but you can take a more moderate position on those which are not accompanied by so many profound consequences. If you understand that teens have a need to rebel, you will wisely let them. You may not like the idea of a messy bedroom, loud music, and purple hair, but as a child psychologist says, "You should be thankful that your teen has chosen to start the process of being independent in relatively safe ways."

※ Let them know where you stand, and then give them some room. There's a lot of leeway in the phrase "I

prefer you don't, but . . .'' It lets your child know your
stance, but it also gives him space for maneuvering.
"Keep your principles," says therapist Peter Cohen,
who specializes in adolescents, "but make it clear you
don't assume your kids will share in them." For example, when they come to you with music and video
games you find objectionable, you can say, "I don't like
it, but I can't govern what's in your head. Please play
it out of my earshot." Your kids are entitled to their
own thoughts, sexual fantasies, and even smashingly
loud music. In fact, try saying, "I find this music distasteful, but that's OK as long as you don't *act* in a
distasteful way."

Of course, keep in mind it's difficult for even the
most careful parent to play censor. You can't always
distinguish "good" from "bad." Although the video
game "Resident Evil" gives its intentions away in the
title and in fact contains Zombies that eat people, many
parents might give a thumbs-up to "Quake"—a video
that sounds like it is about natural disasters but is filled
with people blowing each others' heads off.

✳ Find out what they know and then give them the facts:
Again, you can try "I prefer you don't . . ." but realisti-
cally your "birds and bees" job isn't finished with that
phrase. Since no one has come up with a way to dis-
courage teens from having sex, you want to make sure
your children have the correct information. You need
to know what they *do* know, so you can clear up misconceptions. (And there will be misconceptions.) One
teen was shocked she got pregnant, because she in-
sisted she was on the pill. It turned out she *only* took
the pill on days she planned to have sex.

✳ Understand that teens rebel just for the sake of rebelling. It's developmental. Learn not to take it too personally. If you are a vegetarian, they may suddenly crave Big Macs. If you are attached to your old warm fur coat, don't be surprised when your daughter becomes virulently anti-fur. Sometimes the arenas will be more emotionally charged. Many teenagers routinely back off from the family's religion and become fascinated with other faiths such as Zen Buddhism. Respect his choices, and figuratively leave a space for him in the pew if he wants to return. However, if the holidays are important to you, make sure this is made clear. You have a right to have your needs respected even if your teen views them as too rigid. Keep in mind that a conflict-free relationship is not a real relationship.

✳ Tolerate your teen's hypocrisies. Try to stay calm and say, "Tell me more about People for the Ethical Treatment of Animals." You can express your own viewpoint, of course. ("I see nothing wrong with wearing fur, and you still wear leather shoes.") Just as they question your values, you will question theirs. But hold back on aggressively pointing out the contradictions in your teen's. Otherwise you run the risk of humiliating him and drawing communications between you to a hasty close. He is learning now, and has a right to his confusions. Gentle questionning will do. "I applaud your anti-fur attitude. In many ways I think you're right. But tell me why you think wearing leather shoes is okay?"

✳ Don't overreact. Part of the "fun" of being a teenager is to shock parents. If your teen brings home a real "character," be cool. Remember that friends fill the gap left when teens separate from their families. So greet her new friend, the one with the black nail polish and lipstick and white powder on his face, with a warm smile. Offer soft drinks and disappear. (Actually, that particular look, you may be informed later, is called the "Goth" after Gothic.)

❋ Learn the value of compromise. "Learn how to trade cards," is the way Dr. Peter Cohen puts it. "Sort out what you can live with, like a messy room, with what you can't." When your fourteen-year-old comes to you with complex plans for a day with her friends, try to find parts of the request that are acceptable. Three hours at the mall won't do, but an hour and a half might. An hour at the rollerblading rink is fine, but not at night. Lunch at your house is great, and later, dinner at the local pizza shop sounds like fun. But not at eight P.M. Six o'clock will do. Negotiate and compromise. It takes more effort than bossing, but the results are worth it.

❋ Try to have a good reaction to bad news. Dr. Judi Craig strongly suggests assessing whether you are a difficult parent when it comes to handling bad news. She asks, "Do you explode, give excruciating lectures, or berate your teen when she tells you something you don't like to hear? If so, you increase the likelihood that an adolescent might try to deceive you." If you find that your teen can't tell you the truth because of your reactions, you'll need to let her know that you may be disappointed or upset with her actions (cutting class, for example) but never with her.

Understand that being a teen means there will be problems. Teenagers learn about life through making their own mistakes. (If she sleeps too late on the weekend and is late for work, she will get fired and not have money to spend for clothes.) When she goofs, withdraw a privilege and give her another crack at it. (One little dent in the car doesn't mean she can *never* borrow it again.)

The goal is to maintain peaceful relations with your adolescents. That doesn't mean you surrender. It *does* mean that you carefully choose which battles to fight so that your teen escapes this naturally rebellious stage with as few psychological scars as possible.

✳ **23** ✳

Kids Have a Real Need to Fit In

THE RULE USED TO BE:
It doesn't matter what other kids do.

Our parents didn't pay much attention to their children's need to fit in with their peers. When their children complained, "But all the other kids do . . ." our parents automatically responded, "I don't care what the other kids do. Would you jump off a bridge if all the other kids did?" This reply didn't help children cope with the profound sense of social embarrassment at not being able to do what other kids could do. But the truth is that children of every generation always need to connect with their peer group.

A father shares a story that illustrates how deep the need to fit in can go: "My son is twenty-two. When something goes wrong in his life, if we ask, 'What's the problem?' he invariably responds, 'KR.' We know that stands for Kings Road. We live in a small town, and Kings Road is the main drag, and we refused to let him cross Kings Road on his bicycle until he was twelve. Most of the kids he went to school with lived on the other side. He told us that his life was *permanently* ruined, because he couldn't cross that damned road. The rule made sense, but I never realized just how much it upset him."

From the parents' perspective the rule was designed to protect the child's safety. But to the child, his world was shrunk because of a geographical barrier; the rule kept him from playing with his school friends. Today his parents wonder if they should have found ways to accommodate his social needs better. As his dad says, "Maybe we could have dropped him off on the other side of Kings Road *with* his bike."

THE RULE BECAME:
Teach your child the value of being unique.

Parents today repeat part of what their parents said: "I don't care what other kids do, you are my kid." But they add to that, "*You* are special. You can be different." Parents tell their children to "break the mold," and "be your own person."

But the fact remains that the most important thing for adolescent kids is to fit in as part of a group. Paradoxically, your child becomes his own person only after he feels like everyone else. When teens start pulling away from their parents, their attachment to their friends is part of the process.

HERE'S WHAT WORKS:
Understand that kids have a real need to fit in.

Try to appreciate the fact that your kid wants to be like every one of his peers in terms of curfew, in choice of backpacks, in haircuts, and in privileges. Not that you should give in entirely, but if you are the parent of a teen you will have to readjust your parenting style.

❋ Realize that all teens reject their parents and often their values, so don't take it too personally. Let's take the issue of R-rated movies. If you don't want your four-teen-year-old to see R-rated movies and other kids do, try not to dig in too deeply and become too invested in enforcing this boundary. Some R-rated movies might be OK once in a while. Once your child is an adolescent, he needs experiences that are his alone: "Oh, if my mother knew I saw this movie, she would die." Going to a "forbidden" movie is a pretty safe way to rebel.

❋ Try to see the world through your teens' eyes. When your child complains, "But all the other kids do . . ." he may actually have a point. If all the other kids really *do* have a ten o'clock curfew on weekends and your daughter's is set at nine, you might want to reconsider. When children aren't permitted privileges that other children enjoy, they feel childish.

❋ Get the facts straight. It's foolish, however, to accept as gospel a teen's declaration that "all the other kids are" without getting the facts independently. Often it's wishful thinking on their parts. A mom who has learned the hard way reports, "My son Donald tried to convince me to let him hire a chauffeured limo to go with five other boys to an amusement park for an end-of-year event. He told me everyone else's parents said yes and I was the tie-breaker. If I said no, then the other five couldn't go. I bought it, only to find out when my check was returned by the mother who was organizing the event that all the other parents said no."

❊ Find ways to compromise. Most parents understand that it's wise to give in on issues such as clothes. Kids really live by the expression "You only have one chance to make a good first impression." Kids judge each other instantaneously, and they can be harsh critics who rarely change their reviews.

When her son wanted $43 Levis, Lois's first response was that she could buy jeans for only $12 at the local department store. She explains why she changed her position: "I realize that when my son wears jeans the in-crowd is wearing there's such a 'charge' inside of him, there's actually a difference in the way his day goes." Lois did get her son to compromise and accept $30 jeans bought at the Gap. "It meant a lot to him, and I didn't lose my edge."

Of course it gets to be difficult when your child wants *all* his clothes to correspond to what's "in," and you think his wardrobe is perfectly fine. Dr. Judi Craig, author of several books on teens, suggests, "Instead of telling your teenager that he shouldn't want what he wants, try using a technique called granting the wish in fantasy. You say something like, 'Honey I wish I could not only buy you that designer shirt. I wish I could get you one in every color they make. It's just that it's not in the budget." The idea is not to accuse your child of being materialistic—he is! You want him to know you are his ally, but you are not going to run out and buy him everything he wants.

Don't be too concerned that your teens are learning the wrong lessons. As Lois says, "I could belabor the point about the value of a dollar and that you shouldn't judge a book by its cover and what people wear doesn't have anything to do with their value." But the truth is there will be many other opportunities to learn all that. Anyway, that's certainly not what your teen wants to hear now.

And don't worry too much that your child is not her own person. It's a stage, and anyway, she may be taken to task by the person she is copying. Kids like to be copied only up to a point. They even have their own words and expressions for kids who copy too much—they are called *posers*. Still, most kids would cheerfully trade being an outsider for being a poser.

✳ **24** ✳

Less Is Best

THE RULE USED TO BE:
Less will have to do.

In the past, children were lucky if they got what they needed, let alone what they wanted. There was no real concern about having the most or the best of everything. Less money often was spread out over more kids.

What parents provided may have seemed like enough, but they missed messages about their child's heart's desire. A woman shares her story: "In third grade, when I was eight, Pebbles was born to the Flintstones. It was such a big occasion that it made the cover of *Life* magazine. All of my friends knew they were going to get a Pebbles doll. I hadn't gotten a doll in a really long time, and I begged for Pebbles, but my mother wouldn't get me one on principle. She didn't think kids should have everything they wanted. But it was *all* I wanted for a very long time. It was so traumatic that even now that I'm forty-four, I still feel like I missed out. It was a bad call on my mother's part."

As this woman explains, "You should have some of what you want or you always feel deprived."

THE RULE BECAME:
More is better.

We know of an eight-year-old girl in New York City who has seen the hit show *Beauty and the Beast* twenty-one times, always in a front row center seat. Why so often? Because she asks to go, and her mom doesn't want her to feel deprived.

With more money and fewer kids, most parents can't seem to give their kids enough material things. Children are so showered with things that they are practically buried under the avalanche. And, of course, the wish lists just grow longer because of the influence of television advertising on kids' favorite shows. When a toy like Tickle Me Elmo becomes the newest must-have, then our kids expect to get it. (When Cabbage Patch dolls were so popular that many stores couldn't keep them in stock, some U.S. parents actually flew to England just to buy them.)

There are too many examples today of kids who expect to be handed whatever they want. One mother reports on an unpleasant experience she and her husband had on their daughter's seventh birthday. "We had decided that instead of having presents to open we would take Sarah to get a bicycle," she says. "But when we got to the store she didn't really want it, so we got her a CD-ROM for the computer instead. Except *now* Sarah has decided she wants the bike and even though I said no, she was like, 'I can get the CD-ROM now and the bike the next time we go to the store.' We could see we had trained her to feel she will *always* get what she wants one way or the other."

Treating children as if every day is special and life is like a party can make good times too routine. Truly special occasions such as birthdays can lose their luster. "When Molly's birthday came up in July, we realized that it wasn't too exciting for her to be celebrating with presents, because we give her presents all the time," admits one mother. "When we went to Target to do our errands, we got her a book or a doll. Every time we went to McDonald's she got a Happy Meal. We fell into this pattern when I went back to work. Her father and I both started buying her things all the time. We fell into 'material' parenting to assuage our guilt that we were both working. It didn't occur to us how far we had gone wrong until we saw that her birthday wasn't very special. It was sad."

HERE'S WHAT WORKS:
Less is best.

Kay Willis, mother of ten and a lecturer, says she frequently asks parents to share happy memories from their childhood. In the thousands of responses she has heard over the years, only once did a parent recall the occasion of receiving a material possession as a happy memory—and this parent happened to have been given a piano. What most adults recall from their childhood are gifts of caring, love, and attention.

❋ Keep your eye on the target, and never lose sight of what is really important. The same family whose compulsive gift giving ruined birthdays for their daughter Molly made sure that the Christmas holidays would be special by emphasizing family. "We went out of town and spent it with the grandparents she rarely sees, and all her cousins were there," says Molly's mother. "There weren't a lot of presents under the tree, because we had all made a conscious decision that we were going to do activities instead. We didn't want any competition over whose kid got the most or the best presents." And it was a joyful, merry Christmas.

❋ Each birthday party doesn't have to outdo the "Joneses" or turn into a Cecil B. DeMille production. Here's an example where children proved that less is just fine. A mother shares this story: "My daughter was having her eleventh birthday. I bought a twenty-five dollar game with an audiotape that explained how to run a mystery party. The guests were invited to come and solve the mystery by finding the culprit. Twenty-four hours before the party, I panicked. I knew what other kids in her class had done for parties, and this just didn't seem to measure up. I got on the Internet to find a cooking school for kids. I even ran out and spent $125 to buy a chocolate making kit with candy molds. When the kids arrived, most of them in costume ready for the mystery game, there were six pots of different colored chocolate bubbling on the stove. But the kids were all primed for the original program, and they had a blast. The chocolate burned."

❋ Make sure kids understand the value of what they DO receive. "I believe that the kids should more or less earn the extra things that they get," reports another mom. "I buy them good quality clothes, stuff they are happy to wear, and all the things they need. But if they want something extra like a video game, I try to do a matching fund, so they contribute to the purchase. If the goodies all come from 'nowhere,' how will they ever learn that acquiring things comes from focus, working, planning?"

Yet this parent, who expects her kids to pitch in for special purchases, is candid enough to admit, "On the other hand, there's something very lovely about that generous gut feeling that comes from a sense of abundance. You don't want them to feel this is a world of scarcity."

Some kids, however, do live in a world of scarcity and manage just fine. It has to do with attitude. Do your children think of their toy chests as half empty or half full, so to speak? "We have dear friends who have six children," reports one mom. "When my two kids play with them they are often amazed. My son said, 'They are so nice; they really do share their toys.' I explained they don't go on rampages wanting each other's things, because they figured out that they will never get six of anything. Whenever I visit, I always bring a gift for each child. Often they ignore the names on the packages and just share all of them. Each child has six new toys to play with instead of hoarding his one gift." These are children who appreciate and cherish what they have.

Less is best, but you have to learn to recognize when a desired object represents deep emotional needs. The little girl who didn't get her Pebbles doll is now a mother of two sons. "My kids ask for a lot of things," she says. "I don't get it all for them, but I do try to figure out what it is they are really hankering for, so I don't miss a Pebbles."

✳ **25** ✳

If She Did It, Let Her Pay for It

THE RULE USED TO BE:
Mistakes bring punishment.

Our parents expected their children to always act responsibly. We did our chores, said our prayers, completed our homework, and kept our word, all the time. We did not count on our parents to be there to catch us or mop up our messes.

Although it is a good thing for children to experience the logical consequences of their acts, it's also reassuring to know on occasion that the parent *is* on your side.

THE RULE BECAME:
Put the consequences on hold.
Talk about WHY the child did it.

Today, parents are forever saving their children from consequences. So if your daughter accepts a baby-sitting job and then gets a better offer, the thinking seems to be as long as she *tells* you how she feels, she can slip out of the commitment. And sometimes it's mom who winds up doing the baby-sitting. We are forever doing our children's chores, helping them with homework assignments, and bailing them out of jams.

Late one night, Tara called her neighbor Ruth to see if she could borrow earphones to complete a homework assignment that included taping an interview over the telephone. Ruth lent them to the teen with the understanding that Tara would return them the next morning because Ruth needed them for work. When the next morning came, Tara failed to show up to return the earphones, so Ruth called up her parents. Her dad offered to run out and get Ruth a new pair, adding, "It's not Tara's fault, she went to bed really late and had little time this morning. Let's not bother her about this." Ruth could only wonder, "Why can't Tara be bothered? She's the one who borrowed the earphones in the first place."

Parents have gotten into the habit of being overly involved and rush in to fix whatever their children have broken. They don't allow their children to experience consequences and learn how to deal with them.

HERE'S WHAT WORKS:
If she did it, let her pay for it.

This rule can be tough to enforce because it can both make your child unhappy and underscore personal failure (see chapters 2 and 3). But children need to be taught the natural, logical consequences of their acts.

Here's the rule at work: My friend Meg's son Adam

refused to get ready for school. Meg told him if he missed the bus he was going to have to walk. When Adam finally went outside, he realized how cold it was and announced, "You are going to have to drive me." "No I don't," replied Meg, who said, "It's a fifteen minute walk, and you can handle it." "What if I get sick?" argued Adam, who was counting on his mom to feel guilty and cave in. His mom simply bundled him up, and a very unhappy, slightly cold Adam walked off to school. He was not late for the bus again.

Children need to feel the full brunt of the negative consequences of their actions. Your child also has to learn that his all-powerful mom or dad will not be there to slay his figurative dragons for him. He has to don his own armor.

❋ Obviously you want to offer your child guidance, but it is very important to make him accountable for his own actions and experience the consequences of his mistakes. It doesn't matter how many times you SAY what will happen if your son forgets to bring home his permission slip. The next time he calls from school and says, "Hi, I forgot to get my slip signed and the trip is today," you have to swallow hard and say, "Sorry, but I won't give permission over the phone." (One mom, who knew she hadn't signed the permission slip despite asking her son about it repeatedly, just left the answering machine on, and her son was not allowed to go on a particularly enjoyable field trip.)

"I encourage my children to take responsibility," says another mother. "This summer we rented a house in the country, and my kids took out a glue gun and a new tube of caulking. It wasn't theirs to get into, but it proved too irresistible. They went outside and began gluing and caulking things and ended up breaking the slate cover of a well that had been filled in. I got charged for it. I made them write a note apologizing to the owner, and they missed several weeks of allowance to help contribute to the repair."

✳ You must let your child be master of his own school universe. "My older son is very forgetful," reports a father. "He just has his head in the clouds. This year, during the sixth grade, I have made a point of letting him know that I am not bringing books or papers down to school if he forgets them. On occasion, he's called and said, 'Dad, I forgot my paper. Can you bring it down?' And I've been good about NOT doing that. The only time I've agreed is if it involves other kids, like a group project. I've decided to let him face the music this year."

Here's a common scenario most parents can relate to: Jeff, ten, resists doing homework. Every time a project is due, he puts off working on it until the last moment. This time Jeff has to create a diorama of a chosen climate. Days go by, and Jeff does virtually nothing. After much discussion Jeff finally chooses to do the Antarctic region and gives you a list of what he needs: a shoe box, cotton, and white Dixie cups to help recreate the frigid region. The night before it's due, you see that Jeff has barely started the project. Later you say, "Is everything ready?" Suddenly Jeff is in tears. He suggests a quick trip to a toy store so that he can buy a miniature polar bear. You're about to say OK when you remind yourself that you have rescued him about five times too many this year. "You know, Jeff,

I've been telling you all week to get started, and you ignored me. You are going to have to tell the teacher you didn't do it on time." You wake up at two in the morning and peek in Jeff's room. The diorama is messy and incomplete, but he did cut out a picture of a polar bear from a magazine, and he drew little bear tracks. You have a gut feeling this is not going to happen again.

✳ Let him pay for his mistakes, but you can "chip" in. You want to supply a little help, just to make sure your child can't accuse you of not caring. And some kids really need to practice being responsible. A father describes his son: "My seventeen-year-old son Conner is the kind of kid who, if he has to be someplace at seven, he may not figure it out until *after* seven. Then he still has to take a shower. Last Friday I asked him, 'What are you doing tonight?' He said, 'I dunno.' He honestly didn't know. I told Conner if he wanted a ride to the dance at school I would take him before I left for a concert at seven." From past experience, dad knew he would have to assist Conner; so he paged him on his beeper at 6:00 to remind him to come home for dinner. Conner arrived home about 6:45. Conner *paid* for his lateness by missing the dinner his father had prepared, but at least he got a lift to the dance. As his dad sighs, "That's progress." This dad was willing to take Conner to the dance, but not to stop to get him dinner.

✳ Step back. When your child refuses to respond to your reminders that there is little time left to finish his book report, or that his continual bossy behavior will lose him friends, then it is important to convince yourself that allowing him to "reap what he sows" is a necessary component of parenting. The sooner you let him take responsibility for his behavior, the faster he will learn how to be his own best support.

* When your child does fall on his face, never say, "I told you so." Kids need to feel you support them even when they have messed up. If you humiliate them by pointing out "I told you this would happen" this will only wear away their self-esteem.

* Caveat: Keep reminding yourself to err is human. Do not transform a mistake into a sin. You don't want to turn your child into a criminal with no hope of redemption. It is very important for everyone to be forgiving of themselves. Your child needs to understand that while he should strive to do his best, along the way he will stumble. He should expect to pay the price, but a reasonable price.

Kids must learn to admit and face up to mistakes. Parents can help them see mistakes as opportunities for learning and growing. Real winners occasionally suffer temporary losses. All people learn valuable lessons about life through dealing with the natural consequences: "If I speed, I may get a ticket." "If I don't study, I may fail."

❇ **26** ❇

The Punishment Should Fit the Crime, but Make Sure the Punishment Doesn't Punish You

THE RULE USED TO BE:
Punishment was meant to really hurt.

Parents stepped in and swiftly punished. Often the punishment was the same for every crime—a beating or being sent directly to your room. (Remember—in those days, a child's room didn't have a TV, computer, or telephone.) A child who spilled the proverbial milk probably did cry! She was definitely expected to mop up after herself. One problem was that our parents often didn't distinguish between petty offenses (accidentally spilling milk on the floor) and real crimes (deliberately smashing a glass on the floor).

The child knew if she committed any crimes she would be unilaterally punished without much discussion or understanding of what she did or why she did it.

THE RULE BECAME:
Let's talk about WHY you did that.

Many parents act as if all punishment is, by definition, abusive and harmful to a child's self-esteem. As a result there is a lot of talking about WHY the child misbehaved. ("Tell me honey, why did you feel the need to smash that glass?") The truth is we do need to have some idea of what is behind the act, but talking about it endlessly does little to change the child's behavior. Too often, if the parent is satisfied with the explanation, they often accept it as an excuse that wipes out the need for any consequences. ("We are so proud of you for admitting that you broke the glass.")

The punishment most palatable today is a time out, which is dispensed like a universal cure for misbehavior with the strict prescription that time outs should equal one minute per age of the child. Parents really like time outs because it is a moderate and uncomplicated action that doesn't offend their sense of justice. The problem is that it is overused and often does nothing to correct the misbehavior. There's nothing wrong with a time out for a child who is having a temper tantrum and needs to regain control, but used to the exclusion of all other punishments it becomes watered down and ineffective.

HERE'S WHAT WORKS:
The punishment should fit the crime, but make sure the punishment doesn't punish you.

In general, for a punishment to be effective in deterring future misbehavior, you want the consequence not only to fit the crime but also, if possible, to fix the crime. For example, your four-year-old daughter is a real terror in restaurants; she throws things, crawls under the table, and shrieks at the waiters. You warn her that if she misbehaves now, she will have to stay home the next time the family goes out. When she stays true to form and is a restaurant terror yet again, you remind her of the consequence. The very next time the family goes out to dinner, she stays home with a baby-sitter. She now knows if she wants to eat out with the family she will have to behave.

Let's take a more extreme case. Because Jane knew she would be late getting home, she instructed her nine-year-old son Seth to go directly to a family friend's house after school. When Jane called the friend's house at four to say hello to her son Seth, he wasn't there. It took another hour and a half before Seth finally showed up. It turned out Seth had been playing with some friends and just "forgot." The problem was that Jane was convinced something terrible had happened to her son. Jane's first response, after rushing into the bathroom to throw up from relief, was to ground him for a month, but she later amended that once she had a chance to cool down.

But this *was* a serious offense, which deserved a serious response so it wouldn't be repeated. Seth had been trusted with the responsibility of going directly from school to a designated house, and not only did he fail to call to say he would be late but he was actually an hour and a half later than usual. For the next two weeks Seth was required to come directly home from school and was directed not to ask about having any play dates for that period of time. (As mom told him, "While you were playing, I was sick to my stomach.")

※ Try to design logical consequences. If your son doesn't do his homework, it doesn't make sense to take away dessert. Instead you might limit phone time so he can focus on his work, or make him come home directly after school. If your child breaks an established rule and rides his bike into the street, take away his bike privileges for a week. You want the consequence to change his behavior and to help him connect with the problem.

※ Don't shoot yourself in the foot. When you *do* have to punish your child, don't punish yourself. Consider an alternative to grounding your child if you will be stuck home with her.

※ Don't mete out punishments in the heat of the moment, because they are likely to be inappropriate. If you do get carried away and declare too excessive a consequence, like Jane did initially, admit the need to modify it when you calm down.

※ Don't make a bigger mistake by substituting no punishment at all for a too harsh one. Letting your child off gives him the wrong message. Say, "I blew my cool. I took away television for two weeks. That is too long. Let's try two days."

※ Make sure the punishment isn't too severe. That builds unnecessary resentment in the child. Rather than correcting the behavior, overly harsh consequences only give him the incentive not to get caught in the future.

※ When in doubt about what punishment or consequence to hand out, consider enlisting your child's input. Kids are often tough judges and come up with interesting punishments. They are both humorously creative ("How about no vegetables for a week," one child suggested—quite seriously) or overly stern disciplinarians ("How about two weeks with no TV because I came home late"). Incorporate your child's suggestions when you can, but make sure the child knows the ultimate decision is always yours.

※ You can even shock your kids every now and then when they misbehave. When Susan had trouble at the dinner table with her two daughters who wouldn't stop fighting, Susan took her dinner plate and retreated to the privacy of her bedroom. Then she locked the door. Sometimes it's necessary to turn conventional wisdom on its head. So forget about your kids, on occasion, and give *yourself* the time out.

※ Don't dock your child's allowance as a punishment. There is some disagreement about taking away a child's allowance for being "bad." The general consensus is: If your child does his chores and gets a certain amount of money, he should get his allowance regardless of what his behavior in other areas of his life. On the other hand, if he doesn't do chores, the natural consequence would be no allowance. (Some experts feel that money should not be connected to misdeeds. Otherwise, for example, a child could think, "Gee, it only cost me fifty cents to curse and two dollars for hitting my brother.")

What's most important is to know what works for *your* kids. As one father says; "It's pretty simple. When they mess up, my kids know they lose computer time and TV, because that's what matters most to them."

In addition to levying a consequence, have a conversation with your child to be sure he understands what he did. Improvement of your child's behavior is your ultimate goal, and it is best achieved if he can clearly see the error of his ways.

✻ **27** ✻

Offer Bribes, Sometimes

THE RULE USED TO BE:
Punishment is the reward for misbehaving.

In the old days there were few rewards or bribes. NOT being punished was a reward. As we've seen, children were simply expected to behave. You did what you were told to do. Not to was unthinkable and came with physical punishment. Parents were more interested in stopping the bad behavior than preventing it.

THE RULE BECAME:
If you do this, there will be a reward—also known as a bribe.

The extreme today is a parent who pays her children or buys them treats for every single act of compliance. That is misguided. It's OK to sometimes give a tangible treat, as long as it is targeted for something specific. You should never be "paying" a child for every good act.

Here's an example of a "bad" bribe practiced by a mother who knew her kids got upset whenever she and her husband left the house: "I'll tell you what. If you're good while Dad and I are gone, here's what we will get you." But to be effective, the bribes had to get progressively bigger and bigger. This mom and dad created a culture of bribery. After recognizing how unhealthy this was, the family went cold turkey.

HERE'S WHAT WORKS:
Offer bribes, sometimes.

Rewards can be effective on a short-term basis to nudge and motivate a youngster into a good pattern of cooperation. Any time you offer something extra in order to get a child to do something, think of it as a positive incentive. You are encouraging your child to do the right thing over the long term.

※ Set your reward *in advance,* and make sure it is not always material or tangible. Offering a reward on the spot doesn't do anything in the long run to motivate your child. You don't want him to be the equivalent of a trained seal who only performs correctly if he gets the "fish." You want him to still behave correctly even after you remove the reward. "Thank you, you are a neat kid," can be its own reward.

※ You should never offer a bribe to get a kid to stop doing something he shouldn't be doing. Let's say you have a child who won't leave a party, and you say, "If you come home now I will play Chutes and Ladders with you." That's a bad bribe. The child has the upper hand, because he will quickly learn that if he holds out when he is being bad, he will actually get rewarded. On the other hand, if you tell a child before the party that you will play a game with him if he leaves when you ask him to, then he is being motivated. The choice on how to behave stays with the child.

※ Never let the child pull the reward strings. Take the example of a mother who asks her son to walk the dog or clean up his room and he refuses *unless* he can negotiate a prize or treat. Or a child who gets a point on a reward chart for dog walking and wants to raise it to two points. If you give in, you are being bribed. (Mom says to a crying child, "Don't cry in the doctor's office and I'll get you a Beanie Baby." The sobbing child says, "How about two?" Instead of offering a bribe, this mother should say, "We discussed that you were coming to the doctor today. I'm sorry you are sad. I'll hold and kiss you." Period.)

※ If you positively reinforce good behavior, you may not have to punish so often for bad behavior. If you have a choice between the carrot or the stick, choose the proverbial carrot. A schoolteacher and father of three sons, John explains that accentuating the positive may eliminate the negatives. As he sees it, "Kids don't do as well when confronted repeatedly with *don't*s. Kids always do better when they know what is expected of them. So I always praise them when they do the right thing."

Keep in mind that the potential for bribery is not in the incentive itself but in the timing. When you use an incentive correctly, you motivate a child. You're reminding him in advance that you're going to allow some privilege or treat for certain behavior that he can control. It's up to him. This will help the child learn to do the right thing on his own without prompting.

Life is full of rewards. For instance, you work at your job, and you get a salary; if you do a particularly good job you may even get a bonus. It's OK to teach children about rewards as long as it's not for everything they do.

✳ **28** ✳

If You Are Upset with Your Kid's Behavior, Let Him Know It

THE RULE USED TO BE:
Don't spare the rod.

In the past, angry parents would drag naughty children into the woodshed. They made no effort to spare the rod, and even expected teachers to discipline kids with a ruler. Indeed, beatings, or the threat of one, was the punishment of choice. (In general, parents had physical responses to bad behavior. Talking back or using vulgar language often resulted in having your mouth washed out with soap.) Not surprisingly, kids were often scared into compliance.

In the worst-case scenarios, our parents' actions bordered on what we now call child abuse, and it could sometimes feed a vicious cycle: Children who are abused often grow up to abuse their own children.

THE RULE BECAME:
Spare the rod and talk it out.

Then came the era when any spanking was equated with child abuse. Many studies confirm the notion that frequent corporal punishment can, in fact, spoil a child by breeding mistrust of the parent without stopping the bad behavior.

When push comes to shove, most parents today are uncomfortable with any form of physical punishment. As one mom confesses, "It's just not in my emotional vocabulary to spank my children." (The only exception seems to be if a child is in physical danger. Many parents do find an occasional spanking acceptable if the child is in jeopardy. So if a three-year-old wanders into the street and narrowly misses getting hit with a car, the response is often a quick swat on the butt.)

In general, the rod was replaced by "the talk." Most parents try to find out *why* the child did what she did. Recommendations about how to respond when a child is acting up often focus on what NOT to do: *Don't* let children be afraid of you; *don't* let them ever see you lose your temper; *don't* ever create a scene.

For example, let's say your child is dragging the cat around by its tail. You are supposed to swallow your anger so your child doesn't hear it, put in its place a forced calmness, and maybe send your child (or the cat) for a time out. This means your child may not get the critical feedback she needs to help her understand that some actions, like hurting an animal, constitute unacceptable behavior. If children are to learn from their mistakes, first they need to understand that they made one.

HERE'S WHAT WORKS:
It's OK for your kids to know you are really upset with them.

You don't have to pretend you are not upset when you are truly angry. Parents *do* get "ticked off," and children usually can tell anyway. As one mother admits, "I don't say 'Honey let's talk.' If I'm really angry it's not the time for 'honey.' And he knows it."

You don't want your anger to lead you to attack your child, but it can help you correct her in no uncertain terms. "Sometimes fury is a wonderful engine that can propel you to deal with whatever made you so angry," observes a wise mother. A child psychologist agrees that it is not harmful to a child's self-esteem to know that his parents are upset or even disappointed with his actions: "You can say, 'I don't want to be with you right now because of what you did.' And then describe the antisocial behavior and add, 'Later we will decide what your conse-quence will be.' Rather, it's being wimpy that hurts chil-dren because they don't have any clear idea of what is expected of them or what the consequences are for bad behavior."

However, if you feel the blood rushing and the veins popping in your forehead, count to ten and take deep breaths. Say to your child; "I am really furious. I'm going to my room to cool off. When I'm not so angry I will come back, and then we can decide what to do." This tells the child that sometimes even a parent needs a time out to gain control.

※ Get in control by shifting the focus from the child to your own feelings.

✳ Keep the child informed: "I'm going to my room now, but I will deal with you later."

✳ Once you are alone, find a way to vent. Call a friend, take a shower, jog in place—whatever it takes.

✳ When you are less angry, return to your child, discuss what happened, and come up with an appropriate consequence.

"Distancing yourself for a while shows emotional control," reports a counselor. "You are illustrating self-awareness and the ability to take responsibility for your actions." You always want to model appropriate behavior for your child. You are showing her that yes, people get angry, and then they get over it. And no one needs to ever get physically or psychically damaged by the occasion of anger.

✳ 29 ✳

Let Your Kids (Occasionally) Feel Guilty

THE RULE USED TO BE:
Parents did whatever it took to get kids to behave.

In the past, parents and teachers routinely used humiliation and shame to keep kids in line. In the classroom teachers used dunce caps and had children stand in the corner. We often took the "bad" act of a child and cast a spotlight on it. To give an extreme example, if a child wet his bed at night (which, of course, should never have been considered bad behavior) the parent might display his sheet on the line the next day, for the neighborhood to see. The principle was that the child would be so humiliated by the consequences of his acts that he would not repeat them. There was no thought given to the effect of humiliation on a child's self-esteem.

THE RULE BECAME:
The child should never feel badly about his behavior.

We took off the dunce caps and pulled in the sheets, as well we should. But in an effort not to repeat the humiliations our parents caused us, we have confused guilt and shame and lumped them together. Shame and humiliation attack a child's sense of well-being and cause children to feel belittled and insulted. Guilt, on the other hand, is just the feeling that you have been responsible for some wrongdoing.

As we've seen, the modern way to deal with bad behavior is to say, "Let's try to understand *why* you did that," which doesn't give the child the opportunity to have a pang of guilt about what he did.

HERE'S WHAT WORKS:
Teach the value of guilt.

Many children never learn that there are some behaviors, like lying, that are simply not acceptable. Parents need to instill in children the importance of what *they* value—for example, honesty, generosity, responsibility. (In my house the lesson is Be kind to others. My son often says, "Ya, I know, 'what goes around, comes around.' ")

You can give lessons in values by coming up with hypothetical situations. (For example, "What would you do if you found a wallet in the street?" or "Would you cheat on a test, if your neighbor made it easy for you?") The idea is for your child to consciously choose to "do the right thing" when you are not around to supply him with the correct answers. ("You return the wallet to its owner." "You never cheat on a test.")

By teaching guilt we build the foundation of a sane, ethical, honorable society. Guilt can be like a gatekeeper; it helps children control their impulses.

❋ We need to explain to children, "What you did was wrong." (Never label the kid as wrong or horrible, only the specific act.) Say things like "It was not right to call your friend stupid." Parents often excuse the child with the lame response "Oh, I know you didn't mean to say that." But he *did* just say it, didn't he?

❋ By explaining to your child how others feel, you are teaching empathy, which is the recognition of the feelings of others. Say, "There was no reason for you to tell Grandma that you hated her gift. She loves you and it took time for her to buy you that present. You really hurt her feelings."

❋ Show your children that a good way to get rid of the guilt is to make things up to the person they wronged. ("Tell Grandma you are sorry you made her feel bad." "Go back into the candy store and pay for the candy bar you took.")

❋ Make sure they understand the consequences of what they did. ("Even though it was just a candy bar, you could have been arrested for shoplifting.") They need to realize that their behavior impacts on others and has consequences. ("Because of your lie, your friend was punished for something he didn't do.")

After feeling guilty, the child will probably come back later and say he is sorry. Then you can respond, "Thanks for apologizing." And you hug him.

Guilt is Jimminy Cricket on your shoulder, the nagging voice of your conscience signaling that you did something wrong. Just never paint a big G on your children's foreheads. Even really good kids do bad things, and it's important that they acknowledge it.

✻

Recommended Reading

Are We Having Fun Yet? The 16 Secrets of Happy Parenting, by Kay Willis and Maryann Bucknum Brinley, Warner Books, 1997.

Dr. Paula's House Calls to Newborns, by Paula Elbirt, 1997, available from www.drpaula.com.

Parents on the Spot! What to Do When Your Kids Put You There, by Judi Craig, Hearst Books, 1994.

The Motherhood Maze, by Sanford Mathews, Doubleday, 1988.

365 Tips for Toddlers, by Sanford Mathews, Adams Media, 1998.

25 of the Best Parenting Techniques Ever, by Meg Schneider, St. Martins Paperback, 1997.

Wimpy Parents: From Toddler to Teen, How Not to Raise a Brat, by Kenneth Condrell, Warner Books, 1998.

"You're Grounded till You're Thirty!" What Works—and What doesn't—in Parenting Today's Teens, by Judi Craig, Hearst Books, 1996.

✳

About the Author

Linda Lee Small is the co-author of *Wimpy Parents: From Toddler to Teen, How Not to Raise a Brat,* (Warner Books, 1998), *Be a Great Divorced Dad* (St. Martin's Press, 1998) and *A New Mother's Home Companion* (Dell, 1995) and is a contributing editor/writer of *The Women's Complete Healthbook* (Delacorte, 1995). A former contributing editor to *Ms.* magazine, her articles have been published in most of the national women's magazines including: *Parents, Women's Day, Redbook, Working Mother, McCalls, Self, Cosmopolitan, Child, Working Woman, Seventeen, Ladies Home Journal,* and *Glamour.* She was appointed to the New York City Commission on the Status of Women. She lives in Brooklyn, New York, with her husband and her teenage son.